ADVANCE PRAISE FOR WILMER

"In *Wilmer*, Matthew Callans brings us an engrossing account of the life of Wilmer Arias: a life of extraordinary suffering, remarkable endurance, hard won perspective, and the triumph of choice. Wilmer's example inspires us to bring what we have—our time, talents, and circumstances—under the authority of a positive attitude and a spirit of gratefulness. This challenge rings true; surely we must try, confident that, as for Wilmer, blessings will follow."

**—Lee Huntsman, PhD, president emeritus,
University of Washington**

"Matthew Callans immerses us in a powerful story that takes us deep into a brave and inspirational young man´s life—a man who experienced many tragedies since an early age and never gave up. Wilmer embraced every opportunity despite every obstacle he faced. One of NPH's characteristics is resilience. And without a doubt, Wilmer embraced it. Personally knowing the main character made this book even more impactful; I was even able to learn more from my little brother, Wilmer. I always admired him, and now, thanks to this printed work, other people can be inspired and encouraged by Wilmer's legacy. I encourage everyone to read this book, especially my brothers and sisters at NPH. I'm sure they will identify with his passion, will, and dedication."

**—Miguel Venegas, executive director,
NPH International**

"This book captures the extraordinary details of Wilmer, who proudly celebrated being part of the NPH family. May his journey from tragedy to triumph inspire you and remind you to never give up."

**—Bishop Ron Hicks,
Roman Catholic Diocese of Joliet**

"Unlike others who have written endorsements for Matthew Callans' remarkable story, I have never experienced the personal pleasure of meeting Wilmer and witnessing firsthand the power of his courage and refusal to surrender to self-pity. He was a remarkable young man and Callans passionately portrays the story, a narrative that has captivated and impacted the entire Callans family and thousands more associated with NPH. Wilmer's determination to constantly demonstrate love and sheer joy in life despite the incredible obstacles is a 'Life Lesson' for each of us!"

**—Jim Sinegal, cofounder and former CEO of
Costco Wholesale Corporation**

"With grace and love, Matthew Callans brings us the story of a remarkable man who most likely would never have used that word to describe himself. As a therapist, I wish all my clients could have the gift of clarity that Wilmer's difficult life imbued him with, and his ability to see what truly matters in this life. Thank you, Matthew, for giving us this window into such a possibility."

**—Sarah Swenson, LMHC,
psychotherapist and life coach**

"Wilmer taught us to love life with authenticity and a permanent desire to improve. He taught me to see and live life with an infinite positive attitude, courage, and a contagious smile in moments of maximum difficulty. Wilmer faced his path with a desire to overcome, while showing unprecedented ability to embrace life and all of us who were lucky enough to meet him. With this book, Matthew Callans encapsulates Wilmer's spirit, which invites all of us to find our own path through the power of the mind."

—Xavier Adsara, president of NPH Europe and CEO NPH Spain Foundation

"Wilmer's story captivated my attention and came to life for me in the pages of this book. Wilmer did not let his circumstance become his excuse; he made it his gift, and he took full advantage of the time he was given to live a life with meaning and purpose. Wilmer taught me that life is not just about how we see it, but more importantly how we perceive it. I can only imagine what it would have been like to have met and spent time with him. Wilmer may no longer be with us, but with this book, we all have an opportunity to learn from his remarkable life."

—Zach Tuiasosopo, former professional football player

"Callans fulfills the dream of a truly inspirational young man as he tells Wilmer's story with heart and compassion. To those of us who were blessed to know, love, and be loved by Wilmer, his story rekindles the spark of friendship and companionship we were so fortunate to share. To those meeting Wilmer for the first time, well…be prepared! Your mind, heart, and soul will never be quite the same.

Against seemingly insurmountable odds, Wilmer filled his life with meaning and purpose, and in so doing, became a source of life, hope, and joy to all who joined him on the journey. Thank you, Wilmer, for a life lived to the fullest—a remarkable life, a memorable life, worthy of rest."

—Very Reverend Thomas A Belleque, Pastor and friend of Wilmer

"Wilmer's story of courage and love goes deeply to the heart and core of our NPH family. Seeing life's opportunities through the eyes of optimism, hope, and a deep belief in the goodness of people is a legacy that Wilmer leaves not only to our NPH family and his brother and sister, Jacinto and Yecenia, but also to everyone who chooses to read his story."

—Donna Egge, MA, former NPHI Family Services director, board member, and retired counselor/educator

"As a brother, Wilmer taught me to go through the difficult times. He was an amazing young man who inspired so many people to work for their dreams, never give up, and utilize their natural gifts to find their inner self through the power of the mind. Even though I'm part of the story, I found myself learning new things about Wilmer through the perspective of my brother, Matthew. Wilmer was a man full of knowledge and had a contagious energy about him. This book brings that spirit to life and will help fulfill Wilmer's ultimate goal, which was to help others find their own way through his story."

—Jacinto Arias Canel, Wilmer's brother

WILMER

WILMER

———————————

THE TRUE STORY OF A YOUNG MAN'S JOURNEY FROM TRAGEDY TO TRIUMPH THROUGH THE POWER OF THE MIND

MATTHEW CALLANS

SPIRITUS COMMUNICATIONS

WILMER:

THE TRUE STORY OF A YOUNG MAN'S JOURNEY FROM
TRAGEDY TO TRIUMPH THROUGH THE POWER OF
THE MIND

Copyright © 2023, Matthew Callans

Disclaimer: This book reflects the author's present recollections of experiences over time. Some details have been limited or modified to protect privacy. Other events were omitted or compressed, and some of the dialogue has been recreated.

ISBN (paperback): 978-1-957473-95-6
ISBN (hardcover): 978-1-957473-96-3
ISBN (e-book): 978-1-957473-97-0
ISBN (audio book): 978-1-957473-94-9

Library of Congress Control Number: 2022920381

Edited by Jocelyn Carbonara
Proofread by Amy Weinstein
Cover Design by David Provolo
Interior Design by Jenny Lisk

Published by Spiritus Communications, Hillsborough, NC, USA

In Loving Memory

Wilmer Arias Canel
1990-2020

CONTENTS

NOTE FROM THE AUTHOR

I was humbled in the process of writing this story. The more time I spent around Wilmer Arias and others in his life, the more I became aware of the humility, strength of character, and gratitude that each of them embodied. There's a lot of ugliness in the world, which can consume our minds if we let it. The people talked about in this story, including Wilmer and others, chose to see *beauty*, because there was an equal amount of that around them too. This story shows how we can work to create this beauty in our daily lives, regardless of circumstances.

Perhaps the greatest tragedy of our existence is that we often forget that we have complete control over whether we will make the best of our experience—or the worst of it. Wilmer taught me that we can choose the filter through which we see the world. We can even control the settings.

Are you seeing your life through a lens of limitation or abundance? What are you truly capable of, if you set your mind to it?

Matthew Callans

FOREWORD

As a ten-year-old boy visiting Guatemala for the first time, Matthew knew there was something magical about NPH. While he was too young to put words around his emotions, the tears in his eyes when we left told the story—as did his incessant letter-writing to his newfound friends and relentless pleas over the next two years for our family to return "as soon as possible."

To this day, I struggle to find words that accurately convey what truly sets NPH apart from other organizations. I find myself telling people that they "just have to go there and experience it firsthand" to capture the true essence and spirit of the place.

Matthew, too, was so moved by the work of NPH that he felt compelled, ten years later, to spend an entire year volunteering there after he graduated from college. I believe he was in awe of NPH's ability to create an environment where hundreds of vulnerable children felt loved, cared for, and supported. And he was amazed by the children's authentic desire to share what little they had, and their ability to find joy in everything when they seemingly had so little.

As Matthew's mom, I had no idea that the seeds planted nearly twenty years ago would have such a profound impact on him, but it's been beautiful to witness firsthand. Matthew's life is so much fuller today because of NPH—and Wilmer.

But it's not just Matthew who experienced Wilmer's indelible mark; I can say with absolute certainty that I, too, am better for having known him. This is a sentiment echoed by so many of those who were privileged to know Wilmer.

I'd like to share a little bit of the backstory that led to the writing of this book. This will provide context as you read this beautiful story about Matthew's brother, Wilmer, and the extraordinary mindset he cultivated in the face of much hardship.

Our family's connection to Wilmer dates back to February 2004. Just a few months prior to this, I was in the office of our parish priest, Father Tom Belleque, and asked what I thought was a seemingly innocent question: "Who are these beautiful children in this photo on your desk?"

Little did I know the weight of this question and how the answer would change not only my life, but the lives of my entire family, and anyone with whom I've shared this story. Father Tom went on to explain about Nuestros Pequeños Hermanos (NPH), meaning "our little brothers and sisters" in Spanish, and his connection to it. NPH is an organization that helps transform the lives of vulnerable children throughout nine countries in Central and South America by providing them with love, a family, faith, security, an education, health care, a home, a sense of community, work, and responsibility. This level of care is provided through university- and masters-level education, if so desired by the *pequeños* (children). Knowing how passionate I am and recognizing my love for children, Father Tom asked if I would like to talk to my husband, Pat, and consider joining him on a trip to Guatemala to visit the NPH home while attending the annual international meeting and learning more about the organization.

Fast forward a few months, and we found ourselves on a flight to Guatemala, accompanied by Father Tom and our good friends, Carol and Bob Bubar and Donna Egge. Upon arrival at the NPH Guatemala home, Father Tom immediately took us to the clinic to introduce us to two of his favorite *pequeños*: Wilmer, in a wheelchair, paralyzed from his chest down but all smiles, and his brother, Jacinto, by his side with pride and confidence. We were immediately drawn to their energy and smiles. They were only ten and nine years old respectively, but their connection to one another was quite extraordinary. They seemed mature yet playful, like old souls in a way, yet simultaneously innocent and childlike.

During this trip, we were informed that Jacinto needed a sponsor. We immediately became his godparents, which invariably connected us to his brother Wilmer. Never in our wildest dreams could we have guessed how much these two young boys would profoundly impact our lives.

Pat and I were so moved by the work of this organization on our first trip that just one year later, we returned to Guatemala with our children, Jonathan, aged twelve, Matthew, ten, and Molly, nine—with three other families from our parish. We spent two weeks living at NPH, immersing ourselves into their world and helping out in a myriad of ways. We truly became part of the extended

NPH family during this trip, and our children were forever changed.

For the next two years—as mentioned—Matthew, as well as our two other children, begged us to go back. So in 2007, we returned and spent another two weeks at NPH, further deepening our bonds and love for this organization.

We maintained connections with many of the *pequeños* over the years, writing letters and sending gifts; but it was Wilmer and Jacinto who stole our hearts. They were great students and highly motivated, especially in their quest to learn English.

This was fortunate, because in 2012, Jacinto was selected to participate in the Seattle Leadership Institute, a year-long program where five or six *pequeños* from a variety of NPH homes were selected to attend Seattle Central Community College, learn English, attend leadership retreats, and focus on personal development—with the hope that they would bring their newly acquired skills back into their NPH homes.

We were Jacinto's host family that year, the year he and Wilmer truly became part of our family. Two years later, Jacinto returned to Seattle for the month-long iLEAP leadership program (a Seattle-based organization, separate from the Seattle Leadership Institute, which delivers high-impact leadership training and educational programming for teens and young adults) sponsored by NPH. Jacinto, along with eight other NPH employees/students, were selected from a pool of many applicants to attend this program. Jacinto lived with us once again during that time.

Wilmer, too, had applied to both of these programs. While his applications were seriously considered, his physical limitations made it difficult for him to be selected. His medical needs were just too great at the time. You will understand how great as the story unfolds.

As the years progressed, we continued to stay connected to Wilmer and Jacinto via social media. Often I would speak to them by phone, and then excitedly share any new information with my children.

In the fall of 2015, Wilmer and Jacinto were selected as the guest speakers at the Pacific Northwest NPH Gala. They stayed with us for a week. This was the first time I truly witnessed firsthand, and on a day-to-day basis, the unconditional love and unbreakable bond between these brothers. The care, grace, and humility involved when being cared for—or caring for—a loved one who is handicapped can't fully be expressed in words, so to witness this kind of love in action like I did that week heightened my resolve to someday, somehow, share Wilmer's story. And this is where the idea of writing a book began to take form.

In 2016–2017, Matthew volunteered for a year at NPH Guatemala, teaching English to the *pequeños* in the Montessori program. It was during this year that Matthew's bond with Wilmer and Jacinto took on a life of its own. My family also took a few trips that year to visit our three boys in Guatemala.

Then in September of 2017, Jacinto returned to Seattle for two weeks to be a groomsman in our son Jonathan's wedding, and he came again in December of 2018 to celebrate Christmas with us. Although Wilmer wasn't with us physically on those family occasions, his spirit was felt and his energy shared via numerous Zoom calls full of laughter and joy.

Of all the trips to and from Guatemala, the most memorable visit was in 2019, when both Jacinto and Wilmer, then aged twenty-eight and twenty-nine, joined our family for Thanksgiving—extending into the early part of the Christmas season. It was the first time our entire family was together for this special holiday.

Since 2015, Wilmer and I had continued contemplating the idea of writing a book about his life. I truly believed his story was too powerful not to share. Wilmer had talked excitedly about the idea of traveling more and continuing to share his story while being an ambassador for NPH. Both Wilmer and I knew that neither of us had the ability to write the book; however, we also knew that Matthew enjoyed writing. Since Matthew was intimately connected to Wilmer and his journey, Wilmer decided to ask him if he would be willing to work on this project with him.

So this is where the book journey began—at the dining room table in our "NPH Issaquah" home in November of 2019. The energy was high, ideas were taking shape, and our spirits were soaring.

A Life Interrupted

This story took an unexpected and tragic turn when Wilmer passed away on August 30, 2020. The original plan was to complete this book, so Wilmer could travel the world and share his story as an ambassador for NPH. And then one day, he hoped to open a café in Guatemala with his siblings. This would be a place where people could gather for good coffee and connection—a place filled with books, dialogue, learning, and reflection. The café would provide employment for *hermanos mayores* (older brothers and sisters who grew up in NPH and later lived outside the home), serve as a gathering space for locals and travelers, and welcome anyone eager to learn more about NPH.

The reality of Wilmer no longer being with us was so hard to grasp, because the last time we saw him was in our home on that Thanksgiving in 2019. At that time, Wilmer was in his fourth year of university, studying business administration, and he had recently received a certificate in neuromarketing (a form of market research that focuses on individuals' neurological and subsequent biological responses to marketing stimuli). Jacinto was in his third year of university, also studying business administration, and their sister Yecenia had recently completed her college degree in psychology.

Over the course of their two-week vacation with us, we heard about the years they had spent brainstorming ideas for their future café, and we were excited to support them in this endeavor. Throughout the entire two weeks, Wilmer's energy level was the highest it had ever been. He had no pain, and he was so motivated to begin this next chapter of his life. And we were all excited about this book and the idea of working with Wilmer and Jacinto on their shared dreams. Everyone was primed and ready to go.

Like so many others who knew Wilmer, I was devastated at his loss. I truly believed (and still believe) the world needs more Wilmers, not fewer. I couldn't fathom his absence from my life—or from this earth. I know that the deep pain I felt and will continue to feel since Wilmer's passing is directly proportional to the love I felt for him for eighteen years. I read once that *grief is just unexpressed love.* That resonates with me.

Wilmer often said we were like kindred spirits. We bonded over discussions of the mind, psychology, neuroscience, and many of life's unanswerable questions. He shared his hopes, dreams, fears, and disappointments; but more than anything, he shared his wisdom with me.

In time, the only solace I could take from his passing was that I truly believed Wilmer had become the most Godlike version of himself. I knew that the love he received from Jacinto and Yecenia, as well as his entire NPH family, allowed him to do this. I believe that it was this love which helped him, over time, to perceive his suffering as a *grace disguised*. He never gave up, he never complained, he always chose life, and he awoke to the power of his mind. And then, he became unstoppable.

I thank Wilmer for allowing me to experience God's love and energy through his wisdom, humility, resilience, perseverance, immense joy, and deep gratitude for life. I also experienced it in Wilmer's relationships with Jacinto and Yecenia. Just as NPH had modeled *family* for the three of them over the years, these three siblings modeled it for all of us. Both Yecenia and Jacinto were always there for Wilmer, each taking on different roles and helping in different ways.

As I set the stage for you to begin this story, I want to thank NPH for their love of Wilmer, expressed so beautifully by their unwavering commitment to help him *live his best life until his very last breath*. This book is for our entire extended NPH family as well as anyone drawn to stories about those rare individuals who are enlightened yet humble, and who inspire and bless us with their presence and wisdom during their time here on earth. They are truly angels among us.

I know Wilmer's dreams were big, but I invite everyone reading this book to join me in honoring his life by making a conscious choice: *to change something in your life for the better*. Wilmer can no longer carry his torch, but we can now carry it for him. We can keep his spirit and legacy alive by choosing to be better. I hope you enjoy reading Wilmer's story and find it as inspirational, motivating, gut-wrenching, and healing as I do.

Cathy Callans

1

THE ACCIDENT

"You spent three weeks like this?" I asked in disbelief as I looked at a picture of him lying on his stomach in a hospital bed, bandages covering the area of his spine that was removed during an operation, and iron rods sticking straight out of his back.

"Months," Wilmer responded matter-of-factly and with a grin.

As we began this conversation, Wilmer Arias sat across from me with his chin just slightly above my family's dining room table, gingerly holding a steaming cup of coffee between his palms.

Wilmer had been in a wheelchair since he was nine years old. At the time of this conversation, he was twenty-nine. He was giving me a snapshot timeline of the last twenty years of his life, concluding with the most recent challenge (summarized by the photo mentioned above)—ninety days in a hospital room, face down, thousands of miles from home, recovering from a surgery that was the first of its kind in March of 2018.

Though I had known Wilmer and Jacinto for many

years and was aware of the challenges they faced, the extended conversation we had over the course of those two weeks late in 2019 was the first time they had shared so openly and honestly with me about the more intimate, and often scary, details of their personal struggles and life journeys.

"I was nine when the original accident happened," Wilmer began to explain in nearly fluent English. "The bullet went through my neck and lodged close to my spine, and I ended up in a coma for two and a half months."

I knew that Wilmer had suffered an accident in his childhood that massively changed the trajectory of his life. But until this day, I didn't know many of the details.

The accident itself was nearly fatal, and his recovery required countless hours spent in hospital beds, which created more health complications. Similar to bed sores, wide open ulcers had formed on Wilmer's body as a result of days, weeks, and months spent lying in the same position, unable to move.

A particularly bad ulcer had formed on his lower back early on and continued to grow and aggravate him throughout his entire life. He showed me a picture of the ulcer, after confirming I had a strong enough stomach to handle the image. I looked in shock at a gaping, infected wound that stretched the majority of Wilmer's lower back —a wound that had been festering for twenty years...yes, *years*. Slowly but consistently growing and worsened by his inability to move, the wound became so infected that Wilmer eventually developed osteomyelitis: an infection that begins to eat away at one's bones. The infection had gotten so deep over the years that it began approaching his spine. If it continued to spread, it would surely kill Wilmer within a year or two.

However, an operation in that proximity to the spine

had lethal implications of its own. The specific operation that Wilmer needed had never been attempted in medical history. It would require completely removing a piece of his spine—the piece connecting from his lower back to his tailbone. One wrong move by a doctor, and Wilmer could be killed instantly.

Even if he could find a doctor who agreed to take on this dangerous operation, Wilmer had no way of paying for it. He lived at NPH, in a pueblo town in rural Guatemala with his younger brother and sister, Jacinto and Yecenia. He was completely dependent on medical clinic staff workers who did the best they could with the minimal resources they had. The operation therefore wasn't feasible in the world that Wilmer lived in; his future looked bleak, and the odds were completely stacked against him.

But that didn't bother Wilmer.

"Sometimes to elevate your circumstances, you have to elevate your consciousness…so that's exactly what I did," he told me. Our family was aware that Wilmer was in need of major surgeries during this time, but not the extent of the danger. Detailed communication about such medical procedures was difficult to obtain across countries and languages.

"You were there on the day of the accident, right?" I asked Jacinto, who also sat across from me during this conversation, next to Wilmer.

"Oh yeah," he responded in the casual style we'd developed over the years.

I'd known Jacinto and Wilmer since they were boys. My family became connected with NPH Guatemala, the home they were raised in, through a friend, and an oppor-

tunity to visit that home came shortly after. My parents
were immediately drawn to Wilmer. But they were equally
impressed and moved by Jacinto, as they watched in awe
of the maturity and selflessness displayed by an eleven-
year-old boy taking care of his physically-disabled brother.
Meeting Wilmer and Jacinto for the first time in 2005 felt
familiar. I was only ten at the time, and the language
barrier made it difficult to communicate. But I learned
quickly how much common ground could be found
through body language, smiles, hand gestures, laughter,
play, and food. We spent two weeks in Guatemala on that
first trip, and when it was time to go, we left feeling like
we'd developed a special relationship with the Arias boys.

We kept in contact with the boys over the years
through the NPH sponsorship program. We would write
letters back and forth, share photos of our lives, and talk
excitedly about the next time we would see each other.

When Jacinto was twenty-one, he had an opportunity
to come to the United States for a year as part of a leadership exchange program. During that time, he lived with us
and truly became a part of our family. Wilmer's medical
needs were too great at the time to accompany Jacinto on
that trip, but we kept in close contact with Wilmer through
social media and FaceTime calls.

"Yes, I was there…I was going to sell a hen!" Jacinto
answered my question and laughed. At this time, all three
siblings were living with their grandparents in a small town
in northern Guatemala. "My grandpa had sent my sister
Yecenia and me into town to sell our hen at the market,"
his voice grew more serious as he recalled the day's events.
"A little while later, my uncle came running into town to
find us. He looked frantic and told us to go home immediately."

Jacinto described how, when he and Yecenia got back

to the house, the damage was already done. They returned to find Wilmer lying on the ground, screaming in pain. He was surrounded by his grandma and grandpa, who were applying pressure to stop the blood spurting out of Wilmer's neck.

"How did you end up in this predicament, Wilmer?" I asked, curious as to how a nine-year-old boy could have gotten himself in such a dangerous situation.

"I was a very curious kid," Wilmer told me with a smirk. "So when my grandparents told us there was a deer wandering around the woods by our house, I really wanted to see it….That was probably my first bad decision!"

Peten, a rural town in northern Guatemala, is surrounded by expansive wilderness—and hunters trying to put food on the table. A deer wandering through the village meant there were likely hunters tracking its every move. Wilmer's grandparents had warned him and his siblings not to go outside as the deer passed through their town.

"I left out the back door of the house and followed where I thought the deer had gone," Wilmer said. "I crossed the river and followed the deer all the way past my uncle's house a couple hundred meters away. I saw the deer and slowly got closer, until I was within a couple feet."

Wilmer explained how he looked around and noticed a man standing in the distance. Then he turned around and saw another man equidistant in the opposite direction. As he stood next to the deer, he realized he was caught in the middle. Two hunters were pointing their rifles at the deer, which stood less than two feet from him.

"I reached my objective," Wilmer said, laughing. "I found the deer! But then I paid a pretty big price."

Two shots rang out, almost simultaneously—two bullets coming from opposite directions.

The first one hit the target, collapsing the deer inches away from Wilmer.

The second bullet missed the deer and struck Wilmer in the neck.

Hearing the shots from the house, Wilmer's aunt left to see what had happened. She found her nine-year-old nephew lying on the forest floor, screaming and choking on his own blood—confused, frantic, and begging for water.

The two men ran off after realizing what they had done.

Wilmer was rushed to the nearest hospital, which from Peten, took two and a half hours. The fact that he remained alive during the trip was a miracle in itself.

Jacinto and Yecenia stayed behind with their grandma, still uncertain of the details of the accident and what had happened to their older brother. As they sat in silence, contemplating the events of the day, their grandma described a dream she had the night before. She dreamt that a car had approached the house. When it got closer, a man rolled down the window, and she could see a handicapped boy in the backseat. The man asked her for money to help support his disabled son. When she tried to hand him money, it slipped out of her hand and washed away down the river.

Upon arrival at the hospital, Wilmer underwent immediate surgery to remove a piece of the bullet that remained lodged in his neck, inches from his spine. He had lost so much blood that day, and the operation was very taxing on his body. A few hours earlier, he had been on his feet whimsically chasing after a deer; now he lay unconscious in a hospital bed, breathing through a machine while doctors removed shrapnel near his spine—all from a bullet that wasn't meant for him.

During this operation, Wilmer entered into a coma.

"I was such an active kid," he told me. Wilmer grew up loving soccer, swimming, and riding horses. In Peten, it is customary for children to begin working for the family at a very young age. By seven, Wilmer was working the land with his brother and uncles—farming, and collecting food. He enjoyed this work, and it gave him a sense of independence and responsibility at a young age. He fished in the river and cooked up what he had caught for dinner.

But his first and greatest love was soccer. He played every afternoon with his friends, cousins, and brother—laughing and running for hours like any kid should, without any notion that this ability would be taken away so soon.

The day before the accident, Wilmer had decided to skip the afternoon soccer game with his friends. For some reason, on that afternoon, he felt unusually tired and decided instead to return to his grandparents' house, certain that he would play the following day. He explained to me how strange this behavior was for him, emphasizing that he never missed a day.

Following the operation, Wilmer remained in a coma for two and a half months before waking into a world that was very different from the one he'd left.

"I couldn't talk when I woke up from the coma. I was aware of everything that was going on around me, but I couldn't communicate. When I slept, I had horrible nightmares."

After waking up, Wilmer spent the next month living in the hospital, unaware of the severity of his condition. He slowly regained the ability to speak and began physical therapy sessions with the hospital staff, none of whom broke the news to him that he was paralyzed from the waist down, with limited mobility in his arms and hands. He knew that he was recovering from a serious accident, but the long-term realities of his situation had not been discussed.

"My family had watched me in the hospital, sick and close to dying day after day while I was in that coma. It was very difficult for them to see me like this, breathing from a machine and wondering if I would ever wake up," Wilmer explained to me. "When I did wake up, I could see the pain in their eyes when they looked at me, knowing they could do nothing to relieve the pain I was feeling."

Wilmer's family was angry, and his uncle and grandpa wanted revenge on the people who had done this to him. In the small town they lived in, this was the norm. If someone caused harm to a family member or friend, revenge often caused more damage than the original action. Word of the accident traveled quickly, and soon everyone knew who was responsible.

"My grandpa and uncle would tell me the same thing every time they came to see me," Wilmer explained. "Wilmer, if you want, we will kill him, and we will kill his entire family….Can you imagine being asked this at nine years old?"

"Would you have wanted that?" I asked.

"At the time I wouldn't have cared, but I said no anyway. Now, I'm so happy they didn't take revenge. What would that change? I would still be in a wheelchair, it wouldn't fix anything, and I would have felt very guilty. I am very happy with my life now. I am satisfied. I have met incredible people. I have physical limitations, but I would take that over mental and emotional limitations any day. Without the accident, maybe this is not the case. I decided to forgive; I had to move on."

Wilmer learned that holding onto resentment and hate in his heart would have only hurt his body, mind, and spirit further.

"What is the alternative?" he asked. "Are we just going to hold onto hate forever and create more of it by our own actions? How does that help anything?"

I reflected on how this response from Wilmer was a perfect example of the character he developed over the years after the accident. He was a young man, struck by tragedy time and again, yet continuing to speak from a place of positivity, forgiveness, and peace.

I asked Wilmer what he would say to his nine-year-old self if he could talk to him before the day of the accident.

"I would tell him to be grateful," he said, "that he has been a physically and mentally strong kid. I would tell him to be strong and believe in himself, because things are going to get very complicated. You will suffer so much physically and emotionally, but never surrender. These wounds are going to turn you into a very strong man, wise and generous. I would tell him there will be times when you want to give up, and there will be people who won't believe in you and think you are better off dying than suffering. But be sure, there will be a day when everything changes for the better. You will look back and see that everything that almost broke you and killed you actually made you so much stronger, emotionally and spiritually. Be thankful that you will understand that happiness has to do with your perception of your own life, and *that* gives you power. Happiness is a decision and has only to do with your attitude. It doesn't matter how many bad things happen to you. If you decide to be optimistic about the situation; problem solved! Life throws situations at us, and we get to decide whether they're good or bad. Remember that it's not about what happens to us, it's about how we decide to handle what happens."

After a month of living in the hospital post coma, Wilmer was allowed to go home, still unaware that he would never walk again.

"I was used to doing things on my own and being self-sufficient," he explained. "I liked to play and run around and go where I wanted. When I woke up in the hospital, I depended on someone for everything."

Wilmer was disoriented for a while after waking up from the coma. Unable to move or do much of anything on his own, he was under the impression that this lack of ability would be temporary. He knew he was recovering from a serious accident, and he thought that this was just a normal part of the recovery process.

When Wilmer was released from the hospital, his cousins and siblings were all over at the house, carrying on and playing in the same way as before. Wilmer wanted desperately to join them, but he couldn't get up out of his wheelchair. As this continued to happen day after day, Wilmer came to the realization on his own that he would never walk again.

As I reflected on this experience for Wilmer, I couldn't help but wonder how many times I may have let a loved one down by not being willing to enter into a difficult conversation with them—paralyzed by the fear of not knowing what to say and not wanting to make a situation worse. I can see so clearly now that leaning into my discomfort, saying things that are hard to say, and being present and loving to those who struggle is so much more helpful. Wilmer could have used that kind of love that day.

For one year after the coma, Wilmer was back and forth between his home and the hospital. His grandparents, aunts, and uncles did as much as they could to help, but they had work of their own to do, and other children to look after and feed. Their house in Peten wasn't fit for someone in his condition. Getting around was very difficult without the ability to walk on his own. He developed respiratory infections and ulcers on his back from the operation. They were beginning to grow and become infected. With so many complications, he required almost constant attention and had very little ability to do anything on his own.

With a haunting parallel to the dream his grandma had the night before the accident, his grandparents realized they were incapable of supporting Wilmer in his current condition.

2

NUESTROS PEQUEÑOS HERMANOS

"It's amazing what you can do in a lifetime if you do it little by little. Little things add up over time, and they can become something great."
—*Father William Wasson*

William Wasson didn't start out with the intention of making the impact that he'd eventually have. He was just trying to help a single child in need. All great journeys like his start with a single step.

William Wasson was an American priest from Arizona. As a young adult, he moved to Mexico, where he was ordained and served at a Catholic church in Cuernavaca, Mexico.

In 1954, a fifteen-year-old boy was caught stealing money from the donation jar at Father Wasson's church. Police asked Fr. Wasson if he wanted to press charges against the boy. Fr. Wasson asked the boy what made him steal from the jar. The boy responded that he was hungry and had no other way of getting money to buy food. Saddened by this response, Fr. Wasson took pity on the boy.

Upon discovering the boy had no other family, instead of pressing charges, Fr. Wasson asked for custody.

Over the next few months, Fr. Wasson opened his doors to more children in similar circumstances. He created a safe haven for children otherwise destined for life in the streets. By the end of the year, he had thirty-two children living in a small, rented house in Mexico. His goal was to provide them with proper education, opportunities, and a loving environment to grow and develop into responsible and caring adults.

This rented house in Mexico became the original location of the organization Nuestros Pequeños Hermanos (NPH): Our Little Brothers and Sisters. Fr. Wasson dedicated his life to the organization.

His goal wasn't only to rescue children, but to foster and develop them into productive and kindhearted people. Helping others was a must within the NPH homes, and everyone played a part.

> *"The most important thing for me is that my children practice charity. If they love, they will be loved. This makes your work efficient and effective. Be a positive influence on your own children and on society and achieve your own salvation."*
> —*William Wasson*

The house was founded on four main principles.

The following four subsections include the words spoken by Fr. Wasson about these four principles, taken from his book, *Change the World. Start with the Children* (Wasson 2020). By sharing these words, I hope to give everyone a better understanding of the environment where Wilmer and his siblings grew up. (Note: While he speaks of "boys," this reflects on the time period the content was written. NPH currently also serves girls.)

Principle One: Unconditional Love

So, what is it that makes our children happy? It is, I believe, the balance of four spiritual qualities that have to be applied together. The first one of these is *love*—a specific type of love that the children receive. This is a very important factor in their lives. This kind of love we call security. Our children feel safe because they know that they will not be put up for adoption; that they will never have to leave the home on a certain day or age; that they will never be left to live on the streets; that they belong to and are part of our family.

They know that their brothers and sisters have a home where they can stay together; that they never again have to witness the death of their mother; that they will never have to withstand neglect and separation or be a burden to their grandparents or aunts and uncles. So, the anguish that children bring with them gradually disappears when they begin to comprehend that they have arrived at their house, that they are safe there and that they will stay there.

There are people who disagree with me on this point. They tell me that it doesn't benefit the children to give them too much security, and I agree. But our children have some small insecurities of life in common: Will they have shoes for graduation day? Will they be able to continue with their education in college, university, or technical school? And after so many years with us, will they find life outside the home to be very difficult?

However, they have basic security. They know that we love them. They know that they can always stay with us.

There is no fixed time by which they must leave. They know that the guarantee of their security is love.

In our spiritual formation, we don't put emphasis on ceremonial church. We rather teach the commandments, explain the sacramental system, but above all—above all things—we emphasize the great need to love one another. The word that keeps us together is *brotherhood*, and every child knows that whatever he does against any person, he does against his brother. We teach that the worst sin is not being able to live as brothers. Criticizing someone, denigrating someone, denying help to someone, not sharing with those who need you, are all serious sins. I think children recognize this more and more. It is revealed in their confessions when they feel concerned for hurting or helping someone. Day by day, we talk of brotherhood and try to live it. We remind our children that whatever our race, religion, color, size, intelligence, or location in the world, we are all brothers and sisters. Nationality does not create differences—all men are brothers. If we can accept this, then our salvation and our happiness will be assured. This concept is a reality in our family, so much so that it constitutes a criterion for determining what is right and what is wrong.

Principle Two: Sharing With Others

The second principle in the balance of the four, which together constitute our philosophy, another type of love that children give, is sharing with others.

How do I define the word *sharing*? How do we practice it in our home? We don't give great importance to memorized and recited prayers, because we consider that to be too easy. We believe that a prayer is an action, a good deed done for someone else, and to offer this action is an act of kindness to God. This is difficult. It's easier to approach the altar reciting a formula, light a candle, and place a flower there and say that that is a prayer.

No. In our family, we believe that the only valid prayer is a good deed done for the benefit of another person; that is to see Christ in our brother and serve Him through our neighbor.

Our older boys formed a musical group, and this group goes to the penitentiary of the State of Morelos (Mexico) to play and sing for the prisoners. After the concert, these young men meet with the inmates, chatting with them and listening to their problems. A similar thing is done in the home for the elderly in Cuernavaca and in the hospital for those with incurable illnesses in Texcoco.

Another group of our boys accompany our volunteer nurse to visit a school/home in a very rural area, where they tend to the children of poor subsistence farmers. There, our children share their food, medicine; they give classes in hygiene to the children; they help them with the cleaning and encourage them to study.

Not a day goes by without the poor coming to our door; hungry children; a sick grandmother; an alcoholic; a young mother abandoned with a hungry baby in her arms and another two or three little ones pulling at her skirt. Whichever one of our young men answers the door, attends to the needs of these people as best he can. He simply goes to the kitchen to get some food and gives it to the hungry; gives used clothing to those who are half-naked, gets vitamins for the sick or helps the old grandmother return to her hut.

This manner of sharing helps our children avoid seeing themselves as the center of the universe or as believing that the whole world revolves around them. It's better to see that the world revolves around others. That is why sharing is such an important part in our balance of four principles. With the guarantee of security and without sharing anything, the children could become vain, spoiled, and self-ish. But when we are insisting that you share what you have with others, a balance is achieved.

The child who feels insecure and full of anguish feels a tremendous need to be compensated by the possession of material things. He finds it very difficult to share these things or do away with them. But once the children are with us, even though they bring memories of devastating experiences (some of our children have seen their parents murdered, have lived in the street for many years, have been victims of inhumane cruelties and severe neglect), they gradually realize that they are safe at NPH. Once you feel safe, you are ready to share.

I have never met a happy person who does not share. I have met many different people who have amassed huge fortunes and are willing to share because they give money, but they do it and avoid paying taxes. Certainly, this is better than doing nothing. Others spend their lives accumulating things and money, and when they die, they inherit it all to their relatives or to persons designated by the state, and never know the joy of sharing what they had with the poor.

What is sharing? I think it's giving something that one has, quietly and humbly to someone who needs it. It may not be money. Maybe it's time. Time is something that not many people want to share. They say time is money and it's easier to share a little bit of money instead of time. However, I believe that sharing includes giving our time, our advice, our knowledge, our clothes, our food, our money to those who really need it.

I have found that people who share are the most responsible people. And I don't mean responsible only for themselves. What I mean is that they have a sense of responsibility towards humanity. Responsible people, for example, don't give donations to an unknown cause. They investigate carefully what percentage of the collected funds are allocated to managers and what percentage is used for the poor, whose cause is being used for promotion. After researching dozens of charities, they will find one or two that, according to their research, are doing a good job and optimally using the donations they receive. Then, these responsible donors generously share their money with them.

Some believe that rich people must learn to share, but this action has nothing to do with social status or wealth. It's about each of us. Everyone must learn to share, and the more you can share, the happier you will be.

Principle Three: Work

The children hate to be called "supported" by other people. They prefer to stand on their own and be a valuable element for the family. Once our children understand that we are a family and not an institution, they want to participate in the effort to make it progress. Therefore, work is a vital factor of our philosophy.

The third principle in the balance of four is an old deed that we call *work*. We don't hire other people to do our work. We do it ourselves. We do the cleaning of the house; we prepare our meals; we wash, iron, and mend our clothes; and we do our own construction and maintenance. Our young men dig the foundations, cut the wood, mix the cement, and do everything except the technical aspects of new construction. Also, they tend to the livestock, milk the cows, clean the stables and pigpens, cultivate the fields of our farms, and supervise their little brothers. Our young ladies tend to the babies and the kindergartners.

We are often asked how we develop the habit of work in our children. First, we let them know that the work is often unpleasant.

Every one of the children at NPH has to dedicate at least one hour a day to work. This is above and beyond the time they spend in school, the time for homework, the time dedicated to other activities like music, theater, or sports, as well as the time it takes to make their beds and wash and iron their clothes. The older children have to dedicate two hours a day for work, and the young adults assigned to our offices dedicate three to four hours a day for work. Even our little ones have tasks. Give them an old rag and teach them to clean something. Then when they grow, their chores grow with them. They learn to clean windows, sweep floors, clean bathrooms. Whatever task is assigned, they know they have to do it and to do a good job.

It's not necessary that the adults do the housework for the children. That's absurd. The children have to do their appropriate chores. There is no reason for voluntary workers to make them food, sew, wash or iron their clothes, or serve them in any way. Teach them, yes. Supervise them, yes. Listen to them, advise them, and love each and every one of them, yes. But to do their chores? No! An important aspect of sharing, work, and responsibility for our kids is made as the older ones care for the younger ones.

Children who do these chores (all chores are assigned on a rotating basis) learn to use the bathroom more carefully and advise their brothers and sisters to do the same. All of our children have to do chores that they don't want or like, however, we insist that they have to, and so from an early age they learn the habit of work.

Principle Four: Responsibility

The fourth principle in the balance of four is that which we call responsibility and co-responsibility. We have never had written laws or rules at NPH. Yes, we have verbal agreements, and the understanding of these agreements is that every one of our children will be responsible at all times for their own actions and words. We call attention from time to time about conduct.

If I, for example, encounter garbage thrown on the ground, and I see one of our kids stepping on it, or around it, I call his attention to it and let him know that even though it is not his task, he has to either pick it up or find out who is responsible for it and get them to pick it up.

Our experience has been, with some of our children, that they really like responsibility and can't wait to exercise it. Perhaps to them it implies a certain power or prestige. Others evade responsibility and they don't want to be involved. Therefore, on the one hand we need to channel those who seek responsibility and, on the other hand, strengthen that capacity for those who evade it.

When we see a child so terribly hurt by tragedy, who cannot speak or communicate with anyone and arrives here and begins to understand that he is surrounded by security and love, and then he relates to his brothers and sisters, shares his life with them, and takes his studies seriously because he can see a future, we feel extremely happy.

I think through the understanding we have with our children; they know that we want them to be responsible at all times. They try to be, and if they are not, I ask them why.

And once more, just as between security and sharing, there has to be some balance between work and responsibility. A child that is taught to work, to keep their mouth shut and just keep on working, that child simply becomes automated like a robot. He never asks questions, never challenges anything, never does anything except what he is commanded to do—and that is not good. We have discovered that it is better that the child can speak without fear of repercussions. If he has a logical motive to protest, he should be allowed to do so. They will learn the reasons behind everything.

All children in Nuestros Pequeños Hermanos know that they are loved, and that everyone here gives their time, their energy, and their life to try solving their problems and assure they have a better future.

Over the decades, the organization created homes in nine different countries throughout Central and South America. By 2022, more than sixteen thousand kids would be cared for in the NPH homes.

Wilmer's life would intersect with NPH after his accident at the age of nine.

Wilmer's Early Life at NPH

Peten and the surrounding village where Wilmer grew up had proven to be incompatible for someone in a wheelchair, and the family didn't have the money to keep Wilmer in the hospital for the extended stays he required. One of the hospital workers happened to know about NPH and connected Wilmer's grandparents with the Guatemala location approximately one year after the accident. They learned that NPH had a medical clinic where Wilmer could be cared for around the clock at no cost to the family.

On paper, it was a great situation. There was no question this was the right decision for the family. But this didn't change the fact that a ten-year-old boy was trying to grasp the concept that he would never walk again. And now, he was being taken away from his family.

His new reality felt worse than the nightmares that had taken over his subconscious. Scared and confused, he couldn't understand why something so serious, and so bad, had happened to him.

"My grandparents were the most important people in my life; they were all we had," Wilmer told me. "I was ten! I didn't care about what was best for me. I cared about my family, and it felt like I was being pulled away from them."

The Arias kids had already been abandoned by their father at a very early age. Their mother was unable to care for them, and they were all left to the care of their grandparents. They had very little. An outsider would likely say they grew up in poverty, but I don't think that's how they would describe it. They had happy childhoods. Surrounded by people who loved them, a roof to sleep under, and a rural landscape to explore, they grew up feeling they had everything they needed. Without comparison to the lifestyle and material objects we consider comfortable and luxurious, a valuable life came from having their simple needs met.

Separation from that life would prove difficult. Wilmer's grandparents did their best to explain to him that this was the only option. But reasoning with a child to help them see the bigger picture wasn't easy thing to do. If Wilmer stayed in Peten with them, his grandparents knew he would die. He required treatment and care that they couldn't provide or afford. They saw the decision to move him to NPH as a genuine matter of life and death.

Wilmer didn't make the journey alone. Fr. Wasson

knew that by definition, children coming into the NPH home had experienced some level of separation from family members. He found it important to keep family ties intact to the extent it was possible. Fr. Wasson therefore believed that if NPH took one child into their home, the siblings should all be welcomed too.

Wilmer was happy he would be joined by his brother and sister, but a dichotomy arose in him as he felt responsible for the immediate uprooting of their lives in Peten. He knew that his siblings had no other reason to believe they needed saving from the lives they were in. Wilmer's accident had jarred them out of a life they had become accustomed to and fond of.

The three siblings were separated upon arrival at NPH. Jacinto and Yecenia were taken to their respective sections, or *hogars* as they called them. With boys and girls residing separately, they would live dormitory style with twenty to thirty other kids in their age group in an open room filled with bunk beds over a tile floor. Each child had one cubby next to their bed to fit all their belongings.

Jacinto and Yecenia were both younger than ten at this point, and they joined groups of children their age who had already experienced the transition they were currently going through. Wilmer's brother and sister felt an immediate companionship and bond with their peers, formed by a common hardship and the reasons for their collective presence.

Wilmer, on the other hand, was taken to the clinic—a separate part of the grounds away from the other children, except those who came and went with various illnesses or medical needs. Unlike these *pequeños*, for Wilmer, the clinic became his home.

His condition was very fragile, and on the day he arrived, he was met with immediate concern by Xavier

Adsara, the director of the medical clinic at the time. This man from Spain—though not a medical doctor, but a pharmacist—would end up playing a very pivotal role in Wilmer's life.

In my conversation with Xavier, who would later become the director of NPH Europe and sit on the NPH International board, I asked him to reflect on the first day he met Wilmer.

"When I first saw Wilmer, he was under a blanket, resting in a room with his grandfather. When I removed the blanket and saw Wilmer's smiling face, what I saw reminded me more of a seventy-year-old man than a ten-year-old boy. He was so thin and frail, and clearly malnourished. I could barely hear him breathing, which worried me."

Xavier told the national director and Wilmer's grandfather that it was his professional opinion that if they didn't get Wilmer to a hospital that day, he would die. The modest clinic at NPH was a large upgrade from Wilmer's home in Peten, where he had resided the past year since the accident. Xavier felt that Wilmer needed a full-scale hospital and immediate attention, describing Wilmer's condition as *critical*, which meant that he had been living in that state for far too long in Peten.

As Jacinto and Yecenia acclimated to their new surroundings at NPH, Wilmer was rushed to a hospital in Guatemala City by Xavier and the medical staff. Xavier took Wilmer to several medical centers around the city, but he received the same answers from most. In front of Wilmer, the hospital staff informed Xavier that Wilmer's infection was so serious that it could spread to other patients, and because of that, they wouldn't admit him.

"We went to every medical center in the city that we could, and no help was received," Xavier explained. "As I grew tired and hopeless, I will never forget the spirit of Wilmer as he turned to me and said, 'Don't worry, doc, we'll find another place that will take me.' Wilmer was calming me down when his own life was in danger. I couldn't believe the courage and wisdom I was experiencing from this ten-year-old boy."

Key figures would play important roles throughout Wilmer's life at critical moments balancing life and death. He would meet many along his uphill journey of life, people he considered angels on earth. One of the first, Dr. Fernando Gracioso, emerged on that first hectic day.

Running out of options, Xavier called an old friend of his and explained Wilmer's situation.

"I let him know that he was our only hope after the day we'd had," Xavier recalled. "He told me to take Wilmer to his hospital, St. Juan de Dios, in the emergency area. He said to stay there no matter what they told us—'do not move until I reach out'—that he needed to organize himself and his team, and he would be there as soon as possible."

The third level of the hospital was specifically used by Dr. Gracioso and his team to treat the sick children at NPH every Monday. He did this free of charge, from the goodness of his heart, and on top of the crazy schedule he already held.

On the first day of his new life away from home, Wilmer was brought there, where he would live for the next three weeks as Dr. Gracioso and his team saved Wilmer's life. Wilmer received the antibiotics and care required to slow the growth of the infected ulcer, while getting proper nutrition. Finally, his immune system was brought back to a stable level.

"I am forever grateful for Fernando Gracioso and people like him, unknown to most of us, who give their lives for children like Wilmer," Xavier explained to me. "On that day, I learned the importance of a positive attitude."

Xavier was moved by Wilmer's ability to fight for his life with such optimism in the face of extreme adversity.

"To fight with courage, and fight for life like Wilmer did in those first few hours at NPH and for months afterward, is unbelievable. He kept a smile on his face through it all and shared it with us to give us strength in those critical moments. I have always kept that in mind, that Monday when I first met Wilmer."

When Wilmer returned to NPH, his health began to improve slowly. He continued his recovery and lived in the modest clinic under the supervision of the nurses and staff for some time. Eventually wanting Wilmer to receive the social environment every kid needs, the staff began to train his younger brother Jacinto to be Wilmer's primary caretaker—looking after his daily needs. Then they moved Wilmer into the *hogar* with Jacinto and the other boys his age.

Jacinto had just gotten used to his new life on NPH grounds when this massive responsibility was dropped on him. He'd found friends, started school, and was developing his own rhythm of life. Jacinto didn't have the maturity or emotional intelligence yet to grasp the gravity of Wilmer's situation as he took on the responsibility of being his caretaker.

"I was used to doing things only for myself, and it was exhausting to look after someone else," Jacinto explained to me. "I had to do everything twice now. Wake up earlier so I could get him out of bed, showered, and dressed. His food first and then mine, clean up for both of us when we were done, two sets of laundry, two sets of chores...I took him wherever he needed to be, and his needs came before mine, period. I was just a kid and couldn't see the bigger picture."

Jacinto had no mentors during this time who could teach him the importance of what he was doing for his brother. He was shown the tasks required to help Wilmer physically, but no one prepared him for the toll it would take on him mentally.

"I would lose patience easily, and it made me frustrated. The only thing I ever heard was that he's my brother and it's my responsibility to look after him. He's my *older* brother. I was used to looking up to him, and now he was dependent on me for everything."

This frustrated Wilmer as well. He didn't like being reliant on anyone, especially his little brother. Memories of his active and independent childhood were still fresh in his mind, which only increased his sense of isolation and vulnerability. Also, he was one of only two children at NPH in a wheelchair. Not only could he not do the things he wanted to, but he couldn't do *anything*—even use the bathroom—without the help of his younger brother.

Positive by nature, Wilmer was often defined by others as an *old soul*. But Wilmer saw how much his condition was affecting the life of his brother, and it bothered him deeply. He knew that Jacinto had a life of his own that he should be living. He felt like a burden to everyone around him—with no one to truly relate to his situation and hold some of that pain for him. The weight of his current life circumstances started taking a toll on him, and that spark in him began waning.

"I became jealous of Jacinto," Wilmer explained. "And envious of the other kids at NPH, anyone who could run and play and go wherever they wanted. I pitied myself and asked *why me?*"

Wilmer felt like he'd been robbed of his childhood, and he couldn't understand why. He was only nine and couldn't fathom how a young boy could deserve to be shot. He questioned constantly why God let this happen. These questions tormented Wilmer. He felt incapable and useless, and started to lose the desire to live the life he was left with.

"I even began to think that it would have been better if I had died from the bullet. My family wouldn't have to suffer, and I wouldn't be this burden to others that I had become. I spent years like this. My adolescence was the hardest part of my life. Not only for my physical pain, but because I couldn't find my place in life."

As time went on, Jacinto began to put Wilmer's situation into perspective and recognize his caretaking job as a duty and a responsibility he owed to his brother.

Most kids at the NPH home struggled to find ways to interact with Wilmer. It was easier for them to poke fun or stare, and then run off with their friends without understanding the emotional damage they were causing. So when anyone took an interest in Wilmer or showed compassion in their interactions, it didn't go unnoticed.

When Jacinto mentioned the name "Eliberto" to me, I watched Wilmer's face light up at the memory of the boy. "Ah! *Buena onda*," good people, he said with a smile.

Eliberto was another boy at the NPH home who became extremely close with Wilmer and Jacinto, and he began helping Jacinto with his caretaking responsibilities.

"Eliberto helped me so much and became like a

brother to Wilmer," explained Jacinto. "So much so that a lot of people thought Eliberto actually was his brother and not me!"

Eliberto showed that he had a huge heart and loved helping Wilmer however he could, while simultaneously helping Jacinto. And Eliberto modeled for Jacinto the importance of helping other people, something Jacinto would never forget.

As I listened to Wilmer and Jacinto speak so proudly of these days, I realized it was a time that helped forge their lifelong bond. The hardships they faced together created a relationship that extended past just brotherhood.

"I had so much gratitude and love for Jacinto during this time, and today," Wilmer told me. "He stayed by my side and helped me through everything, and it wasn't easy for either of us. I'd learned how to work the fields when I was seven years old. This formed my character and made me a strong, independent kid who could work hard and do everything for myself. Now I was completely dependent and couldn't even eat on my own. My mobility used to be much worse, and I relied on Jacinto for everything." I could tell how much this experience impacted Wilmer.

"I felt bad for my brother. He was in his formative years of childhood, and he sacrificed so much of that precious time to take care of me. This hurt me so much. I knew he was suffering, even if he didn't say it, and I hate to see the people I love suffer. What's worse is feeling like the cause of their suffering. I cried in silence for the loneliness and sadness that I felt inside."

Those formative years that Jacinto spent as Wilmer's caretaker are reflected in the humble character Jacinto would display over the years. Their collective journey was filled with individual struggles and challenges on both ends. This forced them to create a functional yet beautiful relationship, with a complexity that typically wouldn't exist amongst brothers in their childhood. Tragedy has a way of doing this.

As Jacinto explained, "Taking care of Wilmer during those vulnerable years taught me that his fight is greater than my fight, and I can be an instrument for him to be able to continue that fight."

Jacinto adjusted to life as his brother's keeper. The experience made him grow up fast. He balanced schoolwork and time with friends with the help of Eliberto, who also always made time to tend to Wilmer's needs.

Wilmer, on the other hand, though thankful for his brother's help, remained frustrated and envious—as he longed for his old life back. Still unable to do much on his own, Wilmer watched Jacinto flourish in the community of kids he only dreamed of being accepted by. He wanted to feel like he was included, but he knew he was different, and this frustrated him immensely.

Wilmer shared these words with me: "I wanted to be like everyone else so badly. I fought every day to be accepted, to become a part of the group, to be normal. Every time I tried to earn acceptance, it had the opposite effect, and I would end up feeling more isolated than before."

Our adolescent years are when we begin to form our identities, search for our place in the world, and become a part of groups where we feel like we belong. This became a constant struggle for Wilmer, and his sense of self suffered drastically.

The time period between ages eleven and eighteen was very hard for Wilmer—mostly because he hadn't yet accepted himself. No matter how many positive things he heard or how hard he tried loving himself in his current state, the reality for Wilmer was very complicated.

Wilmer came to feel that the superficial world was key to getting one promoted in society. He was becoming cynical, a feeling that had been foreign to him earlier in his life. With all the social media and emergence of new technology, he started to believe that this artificial world was becoming like the latest fashion, and people were being judged by their exterior as a consequence. This was making it difficult for him to believe that people still existed who could see beyond his physical appearance. He said that he often felt judged and labeled before people actually met him. Yet this was countered with his feeling that essential human qualities that define a person's character are often invisible to our eyes, such as our fears, strengths, hopes, dreams, and ambitions for the future.

Kids can be cruel, often without realizing the implications of their actions. Physically, Wilmer was the odd one out, and for a while that's what defined him. He felt that he was noticed because of his disability, not for who he was as a person. The bright and active kid that he was before the accident felt like a distant memory as he navigated the turbulent waters of social engagement with his peers.

At this stage in his life, Wilmer often felt rejected and humiliated by his friends simply because he was different. He didn't feel equal to them. He felt ignored in school. While everyone played and found their peer groups, Wilmer stayed in the room with no one to talk to or hang out with.

"I wasn't only physically alone; I felt alone inside," Wilmer recalled. The other boys slept in their bunk beds, and he slept in a separate, modified bed in the same open room. With twenty-five teenagers in the same space, privacy didn't exist. He would lie down in bed, and the other boys would play with his wheelchair, rolling each other around in it. They'd fit two or three boys on top of the chair and wheel it all around the room, laughing. He tried to tell them to stop, but they often didn't listen.

Wilmer's wheelchair meant a lot to him, as the only thing that helped mobilize him. It served as his legs, and his peers were treating it as a toy. All these feelings of loneliness and rejection made him frustrated and angry with the world. He blamed everyone for how badly he was feeling, physically and emotionally. All of these thoughts led him to conclude that the world was rejecting him because he was in a wheelchair, and he was different.

However, it was also during this time period that he learned how to be alone—how to be with himself. He said, "Remember this, *being* alone is not the same thing as *feeling* alone. We can be surrounded by people and still feel lonely. But we can also be alone, and feel tranquility and peace with our thoughts and mind." Once again, Wilmer found a way to transform a struggle into a strength.

While hearing Wilmer speak with such maturity and positivity as he continued to recount his story with me, it was easy to forget that he'd spent the majority of his adolescent and teenage years in pain and frustration. It would be easy to read this book and feel uplifted and warm about the level Wilmer was able to achieve mentally and spiritually, and you should! But it should also be noted that Wilmer continued to fight a tremendous and constant uphill battle his entire life. While he didn't want others to consider his state as *depressing*, recognizing his intense challenge would give context to the strength of mind Wilmer demonstrated daily.

3

THINK AND GROW RICH

"A few weeks before my eighteenth birthday, someone gave me the book *Think and Grow Rich* [by Napoleon Hill]. They told me they thought it could help me. In my mind, I thought, *Yeah right, how is a book going to fix my problems?* At this point in my life, I wasn't a big reader. I didn't open the book for a while and went right back to feeling sorry for myself. I was still struggling with many facets of my life: my health, my emotions, my thoughts, my spirit. Internally, I complained and blamed everybody else but myself. I took no responsibility over my situation and still felt like a victim. Deep down, I knew I needed to make changes, and I wanted to, but I didn't even know where to start."

Once Wilmer finally picked up the book, he couldn't stop reading it. It became his obsession for that whole week. He underlined significant passages and took notes on the sections he liked so he wouldn't forget the content. Before reading this book, he fought every day to be respected and accepted as part of the group. This is tough for any child, but even more so for one in a wheelchair.

He went on to explain, "Every group always has the

person who is funny, popular, athletic, smart; everyone seems to have a place. I was never a part of these groups. I never fit in. I felt so different, they could all do things I couldn't, and all I could do was watch. I wanted to do all the same things they were doing, but my body wasn't capable."

By nature, Wilmer had always had an upbeat personality, but his adolescent years significantly challenged his seemingly innate positivity. Seeing everyone enjoying their active lives, laughing and smiling, was extremely difficult for Wilmer. For a time, he turned his anger on God. He said it felt better to hold someone else responsible for his unhappiness.

But he was quick to tell me, "That's when the book told me to *think and grow rich*." This book prompted Wilmer to change the perspective of his life. It taught him about the power we all have within ourselves. The power of the mind, manifesting our thoughts, and cultivating positive emotions. He learned that if he wanted to change on the outside, he had to change on the inside.

This was Wilmer's first experience with anything that could be categorized as "self-help." He began to grasp the concept that our exterior reality is a reflection of our interior reality. He learned that changing his life was up to him. When he made that realization, everything started to change.

After reading this book, Wilmer tried to respect, value, and accept himself as he was. He let go of the victim mentality that had gripped him throughout his adolescence, and he stopped seeking pity.

"When I was reading this book, a very important person in my life taught me that there is a distinct difference between accepting yourself and giving up," Wilmer explained. "I didn't want to just give up and accept that this was my new reality. I just couldn't. What she helped me understand is that whether I liked it or not, my wheelchair was a part of my life, and I needed to learn how to live with that. But this in no way meant giving up or stopping the fight for a better life. It didn't matter that I was in a wheelchair; I could still achieve the goals I had set for myself. I could find other ways to live that would bring me joy." At this point in our conversation, it was clear to me that reading this book sparked the hopeful soul that had become dormant since his accident.

For six months, Wilmer intentionally worked on his mindset. All of his attention and focus were on his emotions, reigniting his optimism, and visualizing himself where he wanted to be—as a man filled with energy, security, and confidence. He began to work twice as hard in his studies. When his friends played, he immersed himself in books and note-taking. Slowly, his desire to be accepted by others was replaced by self-acceptance, and he made his own life his top priority.

"Shortly thereafter, something amazing began to happen. People wanted to be around me, not to bother or belittle me, but to greet me and ask how I was doing. Those who used to treat me poorly and make fun of me no longer did. The respect, love, and acceptance that I longed for came to me once I stopped searching for it. For the first time in my life, I felt accepted by others. I went home, looked in the mirror, and asked myself, *What changed?*

The transformation in Wilmer's mind shifted his whole energy. He was friendlier, smiled more, and was more confident and optimistic. He started to realize that people were drawn to him because of the energy he had started giving off. Internally, he had accepted himself, and the world was beginning to reflect that back to him.

Some of Wilmer's underlined quotes from the book *Think and Grow Rich* are as follows:

- "Every man is what he is because of the dominating thoughts which he permits to occupy his mind."
- "That is one of the tricks of opportunity. It has a sly habit of slipping in by the back door, and often it comes disguised in the form of misfortune or temporary defeat. Perhaps this is why so many fail to recognize opportunity."
- "The most practical of all methods for controlling the mind is by the habit of keeping it busy with a definite purpose, backed by a definite plan."
- "If you fill your mind with fear, doubt, and unbelief in your ability to connect with and use the forces of infinite intelligence, the law of autosuggestion will take this spirit of unbelief and use it as a pattern by which your subconscious mind will translate it into its physical equivalent."
- "You are the master of your own fate, the captain of your soul."
- "First, I know that I have the ability to achieve the object of my definite purpose in life. Therefore, I demand of myself persistent, continuous action towards its attainment, and I here and now promise to render such action."

I couldn't help but wonder after reading these quotes, *How many of us have something inside of ourselves that we have not*

accepted? And how is this impacting us as people? Is it possible that the longer we fight against what makes us who we are, the further away we travel from real happiness and healing?

Wilmer's life seemed to answer some of these questions. He needed to accept himself, because his inability to do so was literally killing him. In our extended conversations, he mentioned multiple times about how negative thoughts toward his situation had detrimental effects on his physical health. He didn't want to accept the fact that he would never walk again, that he would never play soccer again, that he would sit in that wheelchair every damn day for the rest of his life, and he became angry. When he was angry, he became sicker, and his body became weaker. It wasn't until he accepted his situation and owned it that he began to make progress in his health. When he took care of his mental health, he had more energy, felt more joy, was better able to regulate his emotions, and had fewer lingering physical complications. He realized the power that the mind had over the body as he began to understand the interconnectedness of the two.

Through reading the book, he realized that the subconscious mind is always on, always collecting and reaffirming the information that it's fed. Noticing how much negativity, doubt, and anger was present in his mind and in how he perceived his situation, Wilmer started to train his subconscious towards positivity and acceptance. Specifically, he began to meditate, watch funny movies, read incessantly, and expose his mind to *high vibrational content* that would set his brain on fire. That is, he'd take in only the energy he knew would serve him, while rejecting anything that would not.

Wilmer no longer focused on the things he couldn't do like playing soccer, driving a car, or simply walking wherever he pleased. He stopped comparing himself to others, and set goals that would be attainable through his intellect —if he applied himself. He began focusing not only on going to university, but on what degree he specifically wanted to pursue, and what he planned to do with that diploma upon graduating. Part of Wilmer's healing came from his ability to understand the power of his amazing mind.

It was impossible to argue with Wilmer's logic on this topic. It was one thing to hear words of encouragement about reframing our state of mind from a physically capable person; but Wilmer literally couldn't walk, and he would still be the first one to tell us that *our thoughts have complete power and control over our reality*. Hearing him repeat this mantra once again at our home late in 2019 reminded me of the many other occasions over the prior four to five years when I'd heard him say these exact words to me. They never grew old.

The philosopher Gaius Musonius Rufus said, "You will earn the respect of all if you begin by earning the respect of yourself." Wilmer noticed that before he'd accepted himself, people would shy away from him, look at him funny, and not really know how to interact with him. As he reflected back, he remembered asking himself, *How do I expect others to love and accept me when I don't even love myself?* When Wilmer began to love and accept himself, that's what he received from others. He was receiving the energy he was creating and putting out into the world. Up until then, he had experienced the insecurity and denial that he felt inside, which was then reflected in his encounters with others.

The Honor of Being Different

Wilmer's mindset continued to progress, and his positive outlook was slowly recovering. He was adding perspective and wisdom into his operating manual.

Shortly after the profound insight that the book *Think and Grow Rich* offered to Wilmer's life, another significant shift occurred when he was nineteen. This happened when he redefined his perception of what it meant to be different. For so long, he'd dwelled on his inability to be like his friends. He'd thought of himself as less capable, because he couldn't do so many of the things that most "normal" people could do. He'd thought of himself only in comparison to others. This took a huge toll on his self-worth and created limitations in his mind for what he could accomplish. It wasn't until Wilmer stepped into his differences that his own path was revealed to him.

"Identifying yourself as different can be the best thing that ever happens to you," Wilmer told me. "In the beginning, you may have several ups and downs as I did: being rejected by colleagues and received with pity for being in a wheelchair. When you learn to not only accept, but *love*, the part that makes you so different, things will begin to flow in your favor. This change occurs because you will no longer act out of need and lack of love or acceptance, but rather guiding yourself through life with love and self-worth. When you love yourself without underestimating anyone, a healthy love, acceptance, and harmony will radiate from your whole being. Everything you struggled through or suffered from will make you stronger, and if you're looking through the right lens, you will see opportunity in the people and situations it has brought into your life."

In Wilmer's nineteenth year, a donation ceremony was

held at NPH. They were donating wheelchairs to children and teens like Wilmer who couldn't walk. As everyone gathered on the soccer field to watch the presentation, one of the speakers addressed the donors. His words were very impactful to Wilmer and marked another very clear before-and-after in regard to how Wilmer perceived himself, similar to the growth he'd experienced after reading *Think and Grow Rich*. Those words were, "On behalf of all our children and young people in wheelchairs with different abilities, we want to thank you for your valuable donation."

You can probably guess which word resonated in Wilmer's head all afternoon. He went to bed still thinking about that word, *different*—reflecting on why it had such an impact on him. Lying in bed restless and watching the ceiling, he had a conversation with himself: *OK Wilmer, why can't you stop thinking about this word? Why does it affect you so much? Are you different? YES, obviously, I need a wheelchair to move. OK, so what options do you have?*

Wilmer went back and forth like this, feeling sorry for himself and bad about the situation, yet restless and a bit hopeful. What frustrated him was the very idea that they considered him different and not equal to the other children.

"I'd learned that if something makes you feel bad, it's probably not worth continuing to think about it in the same way that's causing you pain. So I asked myself, *How can I turn this around and start thinking in a different way that won't make me feel as bad about the subject?*

"Is being different really so bad?" I asked Wilmer.

"I don't think so. I thought about some of the most outstanding characters throughout history that others admired: Buddha, Jesus, Gandhi, DaVinci, MLK, Mother Teresa, etc. I was sure that all of them were rejected and judged for their ways of thinking and being. But it was them who marked a milestone in history, and we admire them to this day for the legacy they were able to leave, by *daring to be different.*

"*So, Wilmer,* I said to myself, *do you want to be normal and forgotten like all the rest? Or do you want to be the black sheep that chose to follow a different path? To follow the hero's journey, living by my own ideals, and trying to do something to actually improve the world?*

"My response was, *I want to be different.* But if I wanted this, I had to honor the word. I must not only be different physically, but also in how I thought, how I felt, and how I perceived and interpreted the world around me."

That night was one of transcendence and illumination for Wilmer. The next day, his energy increased. It felt like he'd finally released something he'd been holding onto for so long, like a weight had been lifted.

Think Differently to Live Differently

I asked Wilmer what he would say to other people grappling with this concept of feeling alienated for being different. This was his response: "I don't know what you are currently going through. I don't know what is causing you grief or waste of energy, or what you have not yet come to terms with in your own life. But I hope you learn to see the gifts you have within you, that society so often considers imperfection. Maybe you feel fat, out of shape, or you want to be taller or have stronger muscles. Maybe you're alienated because your inner way of being and thinking is so different from the people around you...I have no idea. But what I hope you are learning from my story is that when you start to value and love yourself for the reasons you think you shouldn't, and focus on being the best version of yourself, and become happy with who you are, people begin to value you for being authentic, for being unique, and for being different.

"We tend to be attracted to whatever radiates a higher energy than we're used to, like people full of optimism and conviction regarding their ideals. At times, we may judge others on physical appearance without knowing them personally, so it can be very easy to worry about what others think of us. But this is exactly why it's so important to be our most genuine selves, because it's not about how we look; it's how we feel inside."

Wilmer went on to say, "Have you ever seen a couple that looks uneven at first glance? Maybe one of them is older or physically more attractive or graceful than the other. The common thing is to assume that one has a lot of money, and that their relationship is one-sided or strictly for interest. We form these judgments at a glance, but usually, reality is not actually like this! People are attracted to self-assurance and positive energy, and that comes in all physical forms. It's not about what you look like; it's about how you feel and how you make others feel.

"There will always be people who do not like you, or disagree with your way of living or thinking, and this is normal. You can't and don't have to like the whole world. If you radiate positive energy, your light will overshadow the darkness of negativity and pessimism that others contain.

"People who speak ill of you or others usually are not happy with their own lives. It's as simple as that. Remember that *being different is an honor*. God has given you a privilege. You only have to recognize it, accept it, and love it. Everything will change when you do."

Everything did change for Wilmer once he implemented this belief into his own life. It's why he was able to convey this topic so articulately. Being different was an opportunity for him. What once frustrated him became a way to set himself apart from the pack. He no longer got upset when he couldn't spend time with friends or do all the other normal activities that his peers were involved in. He instead used that time to isolate, learn, read, and grow. He learned so much useful information in the books he read. He felt uplifted by his ability to absorb the knowledge of others and apply it to his life in ways that would make it better.

But as his knowledge grew and his outlook improved, his ego would soon come along for the ride.

4

ARROGANCE, HUMILITY, AND ACCEPTING OTHERS

Wilmer was now twenty, and he was enjoying the fruits of his labor and the dedication he'd put towards his learning and education. He was living with Jacinto in Chimalte-nango, a neighboring town, and taking courses on Saturdays in Antigua, a beautiful tourist town less than ten miles from NPH. Monday through Friday, he worked eight to five at NPH, and on Sundays he took English classes, also in Antigua.

But something else was growing. The open ulcer on Wilmer's lower back in the sacrum area was reaching the bone. This sore had been there since the initial accident when he was nine, but the damage from the ulcer and resulting infections over the years had never progressed to this extent. The cumulative effect of the last eleven years of sitting for long hours had hastened the progression of the wound to a level that was becoming life-threatening. Wilmer sensed things were getting worse and reluctantly met with his doctor—only to hear the words he'd so desperately tried to avoid for years.

"It was so bad that my doctor's advice was to drop

everything—my classes, my job, my friends…. I was encouraged to stay in my room, in my bed, until the ulcer improved. All I could do was rest."

Wilmer was very used to his routine at this point, and now he was being told he must stop everything and further limit his mobility. He struggled to adjust, again. Yet it became clear to him that without health, he had nothing.

"There's no use in having the best job, friends, or results in whatever you're doing if you don't have your health. All of these things have their importance, but without health, you cannot enjoy them," he stated. This period of Wilmer's life drilled this message home to him.

Wilmer's physical condition got so bad that he was moved to a hospital in Chimaltenango. The ulcer on his ·back had caused severe infection around the exposed area. Then he developed pneumonia and other respiratory complications from the spread of the infection.

Wilmer was in constant pain, and this tested his newfound strength of mind and positivity. His thoughts began to spiral, and he got down on himself and his life all over again. As he was reflecting on this during our discussions, he was able to recognize the impact that his negative thoughts and emotions had on his physical condition; but while it was happening, this was unknown to him.

In the hospital, alone with his doctor, he was informed that if his condition didn't improve, he would die within a few years. At this point in his life, Wilmer had made incredible strides from his childhood. He had plans and goals that would be altered severely by his most recent bed sentence. These were plans and goals that had created hope for his life, yet they suddenly felt unattainable.

"I had lost my will to live, I had too much emotional and physical pain, and I was depressed all over again," Wilmer said. All of the progress he had made felt like it was slipping away, and he was regressing back to the adolescent version of himself.

One night in the hospital, they gave Wilmer a sedative, it was around one in the morning, and it brought him a complete moment of clarity.

"I could finally think clearly without pain, and I thought, *Wilmer, what the heck are you doing? You're not like this; do you really want to die?* And I said, *Of course I don't want to die. I am going to live from the hospital if I have to. I don't care that the doctor said I was going to die.*"

Wilmer decided to change the way he thought and felt about his situation, and his body began to respond to that. The more positive he was, the more energy he had, and the more quickly his infection began to heal. He found an excuse to *live:* new goals, new objectives, new reasons to be alive.

"I want to live to tell my story, to create business and opportunity for myself and others," Wilmer reflected.

Something that became clear to Wilmer was that he had to keep his mind busy so it wouldn't sink back into a depression, dwelling only on how bad he was feeling. The hospital staff offered him a TV to have in his room, but he passed and opted for books and a computer with internet.

"I began to download and read books on topics that were new to me as well as captured my interest. Books about emotional intelligence, neuroscience, personal development, leadership, communication, sales, and psychology. I watched several conferences on these topics as well, and took an online course in digital marketing. I was taking in a ton of information, and my knowledge was increasing greatly. But something else was increasing even more: my ego."

Wilmer became arrogant. He said, "The people around me in my day-to-day life didn't seem to say anything of meaning compared to the knowledge I was gaining from the books I was reading and the courses I was taking. It seemed so simple and insignificant how most people around me thought and spent their time. They seemed to complicate their lives with small problems."

Through further reading, Wilmer learned that his attitude and the way he'd been going about things was damaging not only to himself, but to all those he encountered.

"If I really wanted to continue growing as a person, I had to develop the ability to live with others, even if they didn't think the same way as I did. I started to ask myself what I could do to live in a healthy and friendly way with these people. I realized my ego had grown too much from comparing myself to others—but also realized that in some respects it was good, because I had made the effort to learn and educate myself. Knowledge was important, and my self-worth increased as I gained more of it. I felt good about myself, which was a new experience for me."

I couldn't help but think of the irony in Wilmer's story at this moment. For so long, comparing himself to others had crushed his ego, yet now it was making it grow too fast.

Wilmer realized this too as he reflected back on his life. He saw that having ego was good, but only up to a certain point. Problems arose when he became self-centered because of it. When he started to feel superior to others— as if his way of thinking and being was the only way that was correct—he realized he was becoming arrogant, and his ego needed to be checked.

"Once I realized this, I said to myself, *If books caused this, certainly a book can fix it too.* I read *The Power of Now* by Eckhart Tolle—a book about spirituality and the importance of living in the moment in harmony with everyone around us, accepting their differences as their unique virtues, and understanding that each person in this world brings a unique and special purpose."

When Wilmer understood this, his ego didn't disappear, but his spirituality increased. He began to value people for who they were and for their spirit as fellow human beings. Understanding that we are all so different allowed Wilmer to accept that we must all want different things for our own lives.

Wilmer realized that part of what was missing from our society was respect and tolerance towards each other's differences. He believed that if we could learn to respect another's ways of thinking, living, and acting, our coexistence would become more harmonious and friendly.

Wilmer, extrapolating from his personal experience, saw that societal conflicts also arise from the inability to understand different ways of thinking. He recognized that people naturally like to be the best. And they don't like to lose. He saw how ego can elevate self-love, but without spirituality, it can also throw everything off balance. And as a result, people can harm others deeply with their words, attitudes, and actions—if egos aren't tempered with humility. He learned from personal experience how life, just like everything else, is a balance.

Though physically stagnant, Wilmer kept his mind moving and found ways to work towards his goals, even while constrained to the hospital. The extended time spent out of his wheelchair and the constant attention to his health at the hospital put a temporary stop to the ulcer's growth.

Strength in Numbers

We were well into our fourth day of conversation around our dining room table that Thanksgiving week of 2019. I was captivated by his story and the more intimate details he continued to share with me.

At this point, I couldn't help but wonder if there was anything that Wilmer now feared, given all the obstacles he had already faced in his short lifetime. His response was profound.

"With the way that I have to live, a lot of things that used to scare me or that scare most people don't affect me as much anymore—our lives being taken from us at any moment, public speaking, fear of rejection, or being told *no*. These are all very common [fears], but I've found ways to accept and work with them.

"It's not like I don't have fears and doubts. I fear not being able to reach my goals and dreams because of my health. From my perspective, the only thing we need [in order] to reach our goals is our health. Our goals are dependent on our ability to work hard and smart, to have discipline and passion for what we are doing. When I am passionate about my goals, new ideas and challenges give me energy, and that's what helps me move forward during the difficult times.

"One of my goals is to help as many people as I can using my history and life experience as motivation for others. I want to help people find their passions and be happy. My dreams are very big, but I also recognize that the idea of not achieving those dreams causes me some fear."

Wilmer's stint in the hospital put a lot of things into perspective for him. Realizing the power of his own mindset and ambition had allowed him to set goals for himself. Working towards these goals gave his life purpose, and the progress towards these goals provided him with more and more motivation to keep going. This additional motivation had fueled Wilmer a bit too much, however, and trying to balance work, school, personal studies, and a social life had taken a severe toll on Wilmer's health. He was so motivated by the pursuit of his goals that he'd pushed through the physical pain he felt in his body.

While there's honor in battling through physical discomfort, Wilmer's situation became much more serious than that. The ulcer on his back was constantly irritated by the way he sat in his wheelchair. He'd been spending most of his days in class—or in transition, studying at his computer or reading books—constantly sitting in positions that were causing him pain and making the ulcer grow, infect, and move closer to the delicate bones of his lower spine.

Upon arrival at the hospital in Chimaltenango, the doctor had been surprised by the severity of his ulcer. He had made it clear that without a complete discontinuation of the way Wilmer was living, the ulcer would continue to grow, eat away at his spine, and kill him within a few years.

The solitude and inactivity Wilmer experienced in the hospital made him realize that all the progress he had made in his life would mean nothing if he couldn't keep his health. The moment of clarity he experienced in the hospital awoke him to the fact that he had to work on his physical health and progression with just as much vigor as he'd been learning to do for his mental health.

Wilmer was reminded again of a truth he'd had to learn throughout his life after the accident: *a good life is a balanced life, and when one piece is off-balance or neglected for long enough, it can bring everything else crashing down.*

Eventually Wilmer was able to return to NPH—with newfound humility and a deep sense of gratitude for his own life. He also returned with the new awareness that in order to live a long life, his ulcer—and the occasional resulting infections from it—needed to be continually cared for, monitored, and managed. This was the only way to keep it from becoming life-threatening again in the future.

Back at NPH, his physical health became his priority. He had big dreams and plans for his life that were all contingent on his ability to stay alive. Once he put that into perspective, he dove into his physical therapy with enthusiasm and tenacity.

Marta Garate, a physical therapist from Spain, worked in the clinic at NPH Guatemala. When Wilmer returned from the hospital in Chimaltenango, she worked with Wilmer on his rehabilitation and physical therapy. She helped him through several exercises daily to improve mobility and strength in his upper body.

During this time, the two became extremely close and enjoyed long conversations about life or other topics Wilmer had been learning about—an endless list. With other patients dropping into the clinic and limited resources, it was hard for Wilmer to always get the medical attention and support he needed at NPH. At the time, there were more than three hundred *pequeños* living there and only a few doctors and therapists to treat those in need. Yet Marta made it a personal goal to help Wilmer move past his most recent obstacle and continue on with his goals.

Though Wilmer halted all activity and massively cut down the hours he spent in his wheelchair, those efforts went towards slowing the growth of the infected ulcer, not healing the open wound. His physical condition was still critical, and a solution to the most prominent issue was still a mystery. Marta and Wilmer began to research rehabilitation and physical therapy centers for other people with physical disabilities—centers where Wilmer could receive treatment around the clock and where immobility was the norm, not the exception.

Marta found a physical therapy center in Barcelona called Fundacio Llars De L'Amistat Cheshire. Their singular objective was to help individuals with physical disabilities get back to a place of comfortable living and functional movement. Xavier Adsara, the man who was working in the clinic on the first day Wilmer arrived at NPH years before, was now back in Spain working for the NPH International office there.

Marta contacted Xavier about the opportunity for Wilmer, and with their collective network, they raised the funds for Wilmer to make the trip to Barcelona. In 2012, at twenty-two years old, Wilmer traveled to Spain for the first time, where he would live in the physical therapy center for three months.

In January of 2020, When I contacted Xavier in Guatemala to get more of his perspective regarding this time in Wilmer's life, this is what he shared with me: "NPH does as much as they can to provide kids with a second opportunity, but it is up to the child to decide whether to take that opportunity, or throw it away. Wilmer definitely used his second opportunity to grow as a responsible person dedicated to his community and becoming an example for the rest of NPH and kids outside of NPH.

"We see many examples of children who aren't strong enough for various reasons, and fail in their attempt to take hold of this new opportunity and live a new life of love, peace, and dignity. A huge responsibility falls back on the child. The reality is that not many of them have the strength to transform their lives the way Wilmer did. It is difficult when we spend all of our professional time trying to provide for these kids, raise money on their behalf, help try to transform their lives and give them opportunities, and then see some of them throw it all away.

"Wilmer was an absolute light in that department, and he embodied the strength and work it takes to capitalize on a second chance and opportunity."

Wilmer was no stranger to second chances and opportunities. He realized once again, as he had countless other times over the past twelve years, that without the support of NPH, he never would have gotten a second chance at life. He would have lived a short and difficult life in a rural town that wasn't suitable for someone in a wheelchair. He definitely wouldn't have had this opportunity to go to a high-level rehabilitation center in Spain, and he wanted to honor the people who made it possible by stepping into it with everything he had.

For the first time in his life, and for the next three months, Wilmer worked with personal trainers for four to five hours every day on exercises that would help his strength, posture, and mobility. It was hard work, but Wilmer approached it with poise and determination, knowing it could be the vehicle to get his life back.

"The first month was the most difficult and painful," Wilmer recalled. "I had never exercised so much in my entire life. As time went on, my muscles started to gain strength, and my body adapted to the exercises. My body began transforming, and the pain diminished. My respiratory system improved, my self-esteem and sense of security increased, and I began to understand the holistic benefits of exercising. Many times during that first month, I wanted to give up, and I wondered what the hell I was doing there. But there were certain things that motivated me to keep going."

Wilmer's desire to be independent helped him overcome the pain and the idea of quitting. He felt like he owed it to other people to overcome these obstacles. He knew that it wasn't easy to get the opportunity to go to Spain for this intensive rehab, and that many people had done so much to help him achieve this dream. NPH Guatemala, NPH International, and all the sponsors who supported Wilmer in different ways made a monumental difference in his ability to continue his life. His commitment was to himself, and them.

The exercises and support from the trainers helped Wilmer make steady progress in his rehabilitation, but the real motivation came to Wilmer from his peers during this experience. Meeting other people with similar conditions as his, and seeing them fighting for the life they wanted, inspired Wilmer. They smiled and treated other people with kindness. They helped Wilmer understand that despite everything that had happened to him, he was fortunate to be alive and still had a great deal to live for.

Maybe, at times, our own physical abilities shield us from grasping the importance of these concepts and how much they can empower the human spirit.

"My roommate there was also named Xavier, and funny enough, we shared the same last name, Arias. Maybe that's why we got along so well! Xavier made me realize it's not about what you have or don't have, but rather who you are as a person. Just because we were experiencing difficult things like being in wheelchairs, unable to walk, didn't mean we could live bitter for the rest of our lives or had the right to mistreat people around us. Xavier motivated me to keep going on my journey.

"It's important to mention that he was in worse physical condition than I was. I could use my arms and hands a bit, I could move my chair on my own, but he could only move his head and talk. Despite this, he was still funny, smart, and always beat me to wherever we were going...because his wheelchair was electric."

This was the first time in Wilmer's life that he didn't feel like an outlier. For the majority of his life, he was used to being the only person in a wheelchair. Although he'd outgrown the feelings of isolation this used to bring him, he couldn't prepare himself for the solidarity and strength that he experienced from being surrounded by others who shared similarly challenging journeys.

At this point in Wilmer's life, he'd already made huge strides mentally. He was reading books that changed his mindset and pushed him towards positivity and goal-setting, but there was something about the team aspect of any challenge that made the journey more motivating. Wilmer was used to being the one with the short end of the stick—forced to alchemize and cultivate positivity for himself, by himself. For the first time ever, he was living in close quarters with people who had worse physical conditions than his own.

Many people took strength from interacting with Wilmer while he was in Spain. Members of his host family, staff at the rehabilitation center, and other patients at the clinic became quickly immersed in his contagious energy and deep humility. They saw the condition he was in and his ability to remain positive, and they felt encouraged in their own lives—and much more aware and grateful for their own physical advantages and opportunities. It was like receiving a wake-up call to recognize how good they had it, how capable they were, and how little was required for them to feel happy and fulfilled.

Wilmer's experience showed us how *we need our people*. Wilmer had learned to self-motivate better than most people throughout his life, but he hadn't yet experienced real solidarity and teamwork prior to coming to Spain. He demonstrated how we sometimes need others to show us what's possible. Belonging to a group that understands what you're going through, with people who are still there to motivate and encourage you while experiencing their own hardships, creates a bond that has the power to lift people up to even greater heights than they saw for themselves.

In Spain, Wilmer experienced this, and when it was time to leave three months later, he took some of that strength back with him to his hometown—where he would continue the journey on his own.

Wilmer (at right) as a young child, with siblings Jacinto and Yecenia

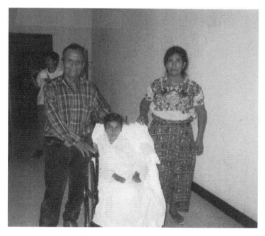

Wilmer, age 9, with his grandparents after his accident

Wilmer with Xavier Adsara, director of the medical clinic at NPH Guatemala

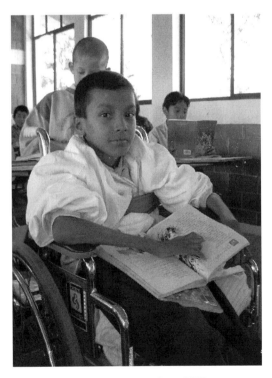

Wilmer as a young student at NPH

Wilmer and Jacinto together in school

Jacinto, Wilmer and Yecenia enjoying time together

Wilmer with Fr. Wasson, founder of NPH

Wilmer (on left) and Jacinto, the first time my parents met the boys, 2004

Wilmer joining my parents at their hotel pool on their first trip to Guatemala, 2004

Wilmer with Fr. Tom Belleque and other pequeños, 2004

Callans family visits NPH for the first time, 2005

Matthew enjoying time with the pequeños, 2005

Jonathan (on left), Molly and Matthew volunteering in a classroom, 2007

Matthew working with older pequeños in an English class, 2007

Matthew working with younger pequeños in an English class, 2007

Wilmer and Jacinto outside the school

Wilmer's high school graduation

Cathy picking up the boys from the Seattle Airport, 2015

All dressed and ready to speak at the NPH Northwest Gala, 2015

Matthew leaving Seattle for his volunteer year at NPH Guatemala, 2016

Matthew visits with Wilmer in his room at the NPH clinic

Joking around with the pequeñas

Matthew with a pequeña

Matthew with David (Jonathan's godson) at his graduation

*Wilmer and Jacinto twelve years later, replicating the initial
photo from 2004*

Matthew with fellow volunteers, 2016-2017

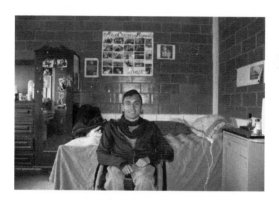

Wilmer's room at NPH

Matthew with all his students

Family picture from Cerro de la Cruz, Guatemala, 2017

Wilmer and Xavier enjoying time together

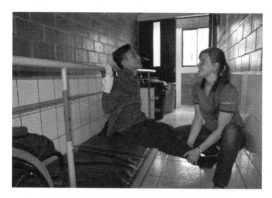

Wilmer working with a physical therapist

Wilmer working hard at physical therapy

Jacinto, Wilmer, and Yecenia

Wilmer's sponsorship photo

Wilmer with Dr. Pedro Cavadas

Siblings at the beach, 2018

Brotherly love, 2018

Siblings enjoying the ocean, 2019

Yecenia and Wilmer

NPH Issaquah, 2019

Enjoying a family meal at NPH Issaquah

Matthew interviewing Wilmer and Jacinto, 2019

Thanksgiving 2019

Wilmer enjoying his wine

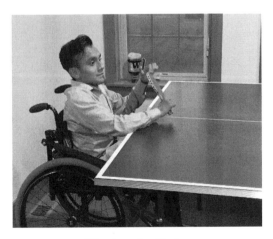

Wilmer's new love, ping pong

Jacinto, Wilmer, and Cathy visit the Seattle Space Needle

Callans family Christmas, 2019

Jacinto, always ready to carry his brother

Alpental Bridge, Cascade mountains

Wilmer's first taste of snow

Lake Kachess at dawn

The NPH logo at the home in Guatemala

The entrance to Wilmer's home, NPH Guatemala

The church at NPH Guatemala

Pequeños were drawn to Wilmer's energy

"God gave me life"

"I didn't give up"

Wilmer reading The Power of Now

Wilmer's happy place: the library

Wilmer, 1990-2020

5

COMPLICATIONS

After returning from Spain, Wilmer felt more independent, secure, and motivated to chase after his goals. One of the first things he did was apply for a scholarship to further his studies in business administration at the Rafael Landivar University in Antigua, Guatemala. He wanted to continue the university education that he'd began, to help set himself up for the career he envisioned.

He was accepted into the program in 2013 at the age of twenty-three. His health was improving, he had more self-esteem, and he started adding more and more to his schedule to actualize the dreams he'd established for himself.

Between 2014 and 2015, Wilmer returned to school and was moving towards his career. Despite the mobility and independence he'd gained two years prior in Spain, he was still having a problem with the ulcer on his lower back at the sacral level. He was once again working Monday through Friday at NPH, while going to school in Antigua on Saturdays.

To clarify, this was a typical schedule for NPH *pequeños*

who wanted to attend university. This schedule gave NPH the support it needed during the weekdays, so NPH could then pay for each *pequeño's* university expenses. To be clear, the *pequeños* were also paid stipends for their work in the homes.

The struggle with this schedule, however, was that *pequeños* had very little downtime. And for Wilmer, given his condition, this proved nearly fatal.

"My only time for myself was Sunday afternoons. This all meant that I was spending too much time in my wheel-chair, and once again irritating my ulcer. I was now in pain constantly and was losing blood daily from the wound. But I continued to try not to let that get in the way of my studies."

Wilmer's active routine during those years made the ulcer grow again. He returned to the doctor in 2016, only to be told the same thing he'd heard a few years earlier: stop all daily activities, and rest in bed on your side or stomach indefinitely. He was told again to leave his job, leave university, leave English classes, leave his friends, and isolate himself.

"The first week of rest was depressing for all of those reasons. I felt like I had been making progress, only to be back in the same position all over again…. In our daily lives, we often ignore the gift that is physical and mental health. We place more importance on external things than we do on our own physical, emotional, and spiritual health. Remember this: our body is the most valuable asset we have. It's necessary to take care of it every day."

Coming from Wilmer, I couldn't help but take these words to heart. The pain in his face as he recalled this phase in his life was palpable. To make so much progress after years of struggle—only to have the wound stop him in his tracks once again—pained me to even think about, never mind to experience firsthand.

Wilmer rested for a few months and had continual check-ins with the doctors. They tried several treatments and medications, but none of them seemed to help or alleviate the pain he was experiencing from the ulcer. After getting nowhere with the best reconstructive surgeons in Guatemala, Wilmer decided to look for a solution in the United States.

Wilmer set a goal for himself that he would find a way to heal his ulcer, rather than just trying to manage it and keep it from getting worse. He believed if he could find a doctor who knew how to close the wound, he would no longer have to battle infections. Up to this point, no hospital or doctor in Guatemala knew how to do this without killing him.

After months of searching, Wilmer caught a break, as doctors in Chicago decided to take a deeper look at his case. In 2017, he traveled to one of Chicago's best hospitals, Northwestern Medicine. He spent two months in Chicago, having a series of consultations and exams. Two NPH donors named Peter and Holly Beres let Wilmer stay with them in their home, and they accompanied him to all his hospital appointments.

The support he once again received from NPH and their sponsors to make this all possible was incredible.

Despite the complexity of all the exams, Wilmer recalled one thing that brought him the most satisfaction on this trip: watching snow fall for the very first time. It was an incredible experience for him, which provided a brief moment of joy before having to face the reality of the doctor's findings.

At the conclusion of his two-month stay, Wilmer had his final appointment at the hospital.

"I remember being in a small room with doctors all around me and Peter by my side," Wilmer told me. "There were two spinal surgeons and a reconstructive surgeon, and they took turns explaining to me in detail that my specific case had no solution."

Wilmer had an infection called osteomyelitis, which was destroying Wilmer's spine via the open wound from the ulcer on his lower back. The only option they saw at the moment was to amputate one of his legs, using the bones to reconstruct the multiple vertebrae that had been destroyed. Then they'd use tissue and skin to rebuild around it, inside and out.

Despite this option existing, it had a high probability that Wilmer would die in the process. The hospital decided it wasn't willing to risk its reputation by taking it on.

"I won't deny it, I was in complete shock. I was silent for a few minutes. The medical team and Peter just watched as I reflected and processed everything they'd just told me. I asked them what other options I had, since the operation wasn't feasible. All they told me was that if the ulcer didn't close soon, the infection would continue to spread. And if the infection reached the spinal cord, I would die.

"In shock, I became very angry and disappointed. I had such high expectations of America. I thought, *How come they can't do anything if they're supposed to be the best?* Most Latinos in some way had come to believe that in the US, you could find the solution for anything. Between anger and disappointment, I got a feeling like I wanted to laugh —mostly because of the hopelessness. I felt like I was between the sword and the wall, and at that moment, there was no other option for me but to wait for death. If I had the operation, I could die, and if I didn't have the surgery to close the ulcer, the infection would kill me."

Wilmer had put all his hope in these medical experts. The consultations, flights, and other expenses of this trip cost almost ten thousand dollars. All to have them explain that Wilmer's only option was to die.

He went to sleep early that night, not feeling emotionally or psychologically well or ready to make any decisions that day. Wilmer had never really allowed himself to think about dying before, or giving up. He had been close to death before, but he'd never fully processed the reality that one day, his wound could actually kill him—until that day in the doctor's office.

"But deep down, maybe even at a subconscious level, I kept reminding myself that quitting was *not* an option," he explained to me.

It Takes a Village

When Wilmer returned to NPH from Chicago, it was all-systems-go to find a second opinion and source a solution that would keep him alive. If Northwestern's doctors couldn't help him, Wilmer was bound and determined to find someone else who could.

My mom spoke to Wilmer shortly after his return from Chicago. She was devastated by the news from Northwestern, as was our entire family. But once again, in true Wilmer fashion, it was he who was keeping our spirits up, rather than the other way around. And she was amazed at his conviction and determination. She recalls him saying that there had to be a solution; he just hadn't found it yet.

Time was a pressing issue, as Wilmer's condition was growing worse by the day. He knew the clock was ticking, and any time wasted inched him closer to his seemingly inevitable fate. The NPH foundation pooled resources, called every hospital they could think of, and tried to keep a brave and hopeful outlook for Wilmer, despite the dire situation.

The operation he required had never been attempted in medical history, so it wasn't surprising that they were denied by every hospital they contacted. Wilmer, once again, was balancing a thin line between life and death. All of their efforts only confirmed the fact that Wilmer had no option other than to wait out his remaining time on earth in pain.

Then, right when things seemed completely hopeless, Marta Garate, the physical therapist who had worked so closely with Wilmer in the clinic, remembered a very important person from her past:

Years prior, Marta had applied for a position to go on medical service trips with a doctor she had learned about through a friend. His name was Pedro Cavadas. Every year, Dr. Cavadas would perform free surgeries in impover-ished countries that didn't have the ability or resources to provide health care.

Marta was accepted and went on one of these trips with him to Tanzania. She described it as an eye-opening experience. Her learning curve was steep, and she expressed how difficult it was to see the condition that some of these people were in and the minimal health care they had access to. She recalled seeing things there that one would only hear about in the movies, including one boy who had most of his leg chewed off by a lion. Dr. Cavadas provided all the equipment and did as many operations as he could for those people, all free of charge.

In Guatemala, they didn't know what to do with Wilmer's ulcer. All of the suggestions felt illogical, and most hospitals didn't even have the resources to perform the operation Wilmer required. Marta thought to reach out to Dr. Cavadas when they were running out of options for Wilmer.

Marta connected to Dr. Cavadas via email, explaining Wilmer's situation. It had been years since she'd interacted with him. She let him know that they had exhausted almost all of their options and were beginning to lose hope. Pedro Cavadas performed thousands of surgeries all over the world every single year. The chances he would respond, or even remember her from the Tanzania trip, were small, and Marta didn't get her hopes up when she reached out.

But on the same day she contacted Dr. Cavadas, she received a simple response: "Bring him to Spain."

"I couldn't believe it," Marta told me when I reached out to her about the exchange. "I didn't even think I was going to get a response, so to receive that message back so quickly felt like a cosmic occurrence."

"I was speechless," Wilmer told me. Though he'd been manifesting a solution with his thoughts and energy for months, deep down Wilmer knew his condition was dire.

"I had become so used to hearing *no, it's too difficult, it isn't possible*. With Dr. Cavadas, I believed we had finally found the man who could actually save my life," Wilmer said as his eyes welled up with tears.

The NPH International community moved fast. With the help of Xavier and Marta, they connected with a family in Spain that had a house Wilmer could stay in for as long as he needed to before and after the surgeries. The house belonged to Jaime Cassanova.

Wilmer traveled to Spain on a long redeye flight from Guatemala—enduring excruciating pain.

"The first time I saw him was at the airport exit doors when he came through in his wheelchair," Jaime told me. He wore a hooded sweatshirt pulled over his head and looked exhausted and depleted, but relieved to have finally arrived. When I met him, he raised his head and greeted me with a wonderful smile."

At this point, all Wilmer wanted to do was lay down and rest. But in typical Wilmer fashion, he first offered Jaime a huge smile and a warm hello.

"I saw the look of pain on his face," recalls Jaime, "but I also saw pure hope. I could tell he was a fighter, and I admired him from the first moment I saw him. His humility, gratitude, and kindness radiated out of all the pores in his body."

Wilmer slept and regained his strength. The next day, he went in to meet Dr. Pedro Cavadas for the first time. Coming off his experience in Chicago, Wilmer was used to medical professionals expressing doubt about his future and being dumbfounded by his physical circumstance. Although his confidence took a big hit in Chicago, his hope never truly subsided.

When he met Dr. Cavadas, he was so grateful to have finally connected with someone who matched his belief that his dire situation truly did have a solution. He showed strong and positive energy towards Wilmer in their interactions. He was also upfront about the risks involved and made sure Wilmer had a complete understanding of the operations.

One thing that stood out to Wilmer was that Dr. Cavadas never mentioned the word *impossible* when describing what needed to be done. After briefing Wilmer on everything that was damaged in his body—and everything that needed to be removed, shifted, cut, replaced, and sewn together—he concluded by telling Wilmer, "It's an absolute miracle that you're even alive at this point, and in the physical condition you're in right now. You should already be dead."

"Well, yeah," Wilmer replied, "what the heck do you think I'm doing here?"

❧

Wilmer returned to Jaime's house (which in Wilmer's words, was "awesome") to prepare for his surgery in a few days. In that time, Jaime got to know Wilmer and quickly became fascinated and moved by everything he had to say. For a young man facing what Wilmer was about to take on, Jaime expected a nervous wreck. But what he experienced was the polar opposite. Jaime connected with Wilmer immediately, captivated by his serenity and quiet self-confidence. Despite the fact that Wilmer's life had been one of continuous suffering, he transmitted inner peace, compassion for others, and a humility that made one reflect on their own life.

"Talking with Wilmer is always transcendental, almost spiritual," Jaime later reflected. "I believe in human beings and their goodness, and I believe we only have to be ourselves to find peace. With Wilmer, it was always like that. It flows, it's easy, it makes you think that everything in life can be achieved. You just have to be consistent."

Jaime also loved Wilmer's sense of humor, and how he always appeared to be happy and hopeful.

"Even when the pain was devouring him inside, he never reflected it. He was generous and grateful, with a keen ability to put himself in other people's shoes. The time I spent with him in Spain made me self-reflect on what's truly important in my life…certainly not material possessions," Jaime said with a smile.

One afternoon during Wilmer's stay, before the operation, Jaime invited many of his friends over to meet Wilmer, including adults and children. Wilmer got dressed up and greeted people one by one at the door in his wheel-chair, with a smile as always. Everyone made a circle around him and began asking questions about his life. Little by little, the atmosphere became more and more intimate.

"We felt relaxed. We laughed with him and became aware of his situation and the strength he had," said Jaime. "At one point, someone asked him if he didn't mind talking about the accident. With a smile, he began to speak, and detail by detail replayed the events of his life. I noticed my friends' faces beginning to change as they listened."

Jaime explained how it was impossible to listen to Wilmer and not be confronted by all the unimportant things you'd assign value to in your own life. Wilmer conveyed his story with uncommon naturalness, good sense, and admirable humility as always.

"We all ended up crying and even laughing out loud," remembered Jaime. "He always managed to give a touch of humor to his hard moments. What great lessons we all learned that afternoon. Everyone left with such admiration and hope for Wilmer. They thanked him deeply for sharing those moments from his life. That was Wilmer: simple, sensible, honest, humble, and enthusiastic."

These are characteristics anyone would hope to display on a good day. Wilmer was days away from a reconstructive surgery that could end his life, yet he was still emulating strength and enthusiasm, radiating light and positive energy.

The Surgeries

In March of 2018, Wilmer went in for his first surgery with Dr. Cavadas. The seven-hour operation would leave zero room for error.

This surgery would remove the vertebrae in Wilmer's spine that had been destroyed by the infected ulcer. Essentially, the entire stretch of Wilmer's spine from the midpoint to the tailbone had been completely eaten away by the ulcer. This included his lumbar vertebrae, all the vertebrae from his sacrum, and his coccyx. After removing the damaged pieces of the spine, they would cleanse the rest of the infected area with powerful antibiotics. Once the bones from the spine were removed, the missing part would be replaced with irons that acted as placeholders until the next surgery Wilmer required.

As our conversation about Wilmer's life story progressed that Thanksgiving week, I asked Wilmer about his mindset leading up to those daunting surgeries.

"Before surgery I felt a little bit excited, a little nervous, and a little bit resigned," Wilmer told me.

Wilmer was excited that eight months after being in the United States, the opportunity he'd been wanting had finally come up. He was also nervous, because the operations weren't going to be simple, and he was risking his life. And he was resigned because of how many *no's* he'd heard until that point.

"It would no longer be strange if I went there and found out my case was impossible to deal with," he explained. "I had also already accepted that if I died during surgery, I would be satisfied and know that I died fighting for what I wanted."

Wilmer was also very grateful for the people who played a part in giving him the opportunity to travel back to Spain and undergo the operations, explaining, "I am only a result of the kindness and love of so many people. I owe all of them for my opportunity to stay alive."

Wilmer never missed an opportunity to find humor and make others smile. When he came out of the operating room after his first surgery, Jaime asked him how he was feeling and if he was happy that it was over with. Even with the anesthesia and iron rods holding his spine together, he responded with a smirk and told Jaime that he felt *Spanish*. From the blood transfusion, Wilmer now had Spaniard blood flowing through his veins! Imagine in that hard moment, making a joke.

"It made us laugh out loud," Jaime told me. "*What an incredible young man*, I thought. I was overwhelmed with admiration."

Wilmer spent a week in the hospital bed recovering from the first operation. When he could sit up on his own, they sent him back to Jaime's house to rest, regain his strength, and prepare for the second operation.

The second surgery would create a bridge that connected Wilmer's pelvis to the part that had been removed in the first surgery.

"That space in my spine was empty, I was literally broken in two! Doctor Cavadas had to rejoin the pieces of my skeleton that had been removed. Dr. Cavadas is a genius. It occurred to him to use the fibula bone of my right leg to rejoin my spine and pelvis, without amputating my leg," Wilmer recalled.

This second surgery lasted nine hours in the operating room. Dr. Cavadas used iron to secure Wilmer's spine to his pelvis. He also used portions of the tissue and skin of Wilmer's right leg to cover the hole in his lower back where the ulcer had been.

Wilmer told me that this was the most painful and

complicated surgery of his life. The pain when he woke up in the recovery room was excruciating, unbearable, and seemingly endless. The painkillers they gave him weren't enough. He was supposed to remain on his stomach for three weeks until the full process of recovery was complete in his body. He went several days without being able to eat or drink anything on his own. They fed him through an IV as all he could do was lay there on his stomach. "I had trouble breathing, I couldn't sleep, my neck and shoulders hurt, and overall I was in pain everywhere. It was horrible," Wilmer said.

One day before the end of that three-week recovery period, one of the irons in Wilmer's back became infected, which created another large wound around it. Wilmer had to return to the operating room for a third emergency surgery to remove the pieces of iron and disinfect the entire area.

"The three weeks I was supposed to be in the hospital turned into three months."

After a weeklong recovery from the emergency third surgery, they sent Wilmer back to Jaime's house in Spain to rest and be close enough to the hospital for monitoring. For two months, Wilmer stayed there, periodically returning to the hospital for x-rays and check-ups. Even at Jaime's, Wilmer had to lie face down all hours of the day.

After two months of recovery, he returned to the hospital to see how everything was going with his healing. Fortunately, everything had settled into place inside Wilmer's body, and he could finally sit up with the help of a corset that kept his spine straight and firm.

"My life was changed. For the first time in twenty years, I could sit without pain. Up until these surgeries, my wound was always open and in need of daily care. The rubbing from sitting in my wheelchair always created pain.

Now, my ulcer was closed and no longer exposed to infection. I no longer needed to readjust my position constantly to find some comfort. I was the happiest man in the world."

In the remaining time that Wilmer spent in Spain recovering, Jaime got to know him on an even deeper level. He was increasingly moved by Wilmer's character, strength, and wisdom. When I asked Jaime to reflect on the impact Wilmer had made on his life, this was his response: "To be with Wilmer was to be in peace. He made me bigger inside. Knowing him taught me to value small things, small gestures, and gave importance to things that really matter. He taught me what it means and what it looks like to literally fight for life. I have had a relatively easy life, and I think that took away the passion for a lot of things. Wilmer taught by example to be humble, to feel comfortable with oneself, and above all, to love from within —without conditions, without deception, without lies.

"His passage through my life has made me reflect on: *Why are we here in this world, and what really matters?*" Jaime added. Not material things, not what society sells to make you believe you need what you do not. He taught me to go back to the basics. Love yourself and be honest with others. By his example and his presence, he changed the world around him. His simplicity, humility, passion, and strength are the energy we need to move this world and take us back to the essence of human beings: love.

"I would have liked to take Wilmer for a walk in a thousand different places," Jaime reflected. "I wanted him to see everything. With him, I felt the importance of the little things that we all take for granted. Our lives went down very different paths, but we remained friends who spoke to each other from the heart, and laughed at nonsense. Wilmer was an inspiration and left a mark every-where he went. He changed the world around him."

Wilmer spent most of his recovery time reading, listening to uplifting speakers, and watching good energy movies. But during this time, something arose in him that felt like regret. He didn't regret the things he'd done, but rather the things he could have done but never dared to do. He regretted that his fear had kept him from doing some things he liked.

"I decided that if I live, I will live doing what I'm passionate about," Wilmer shared with me. "Even if during the process I felt ashamed, sad, or afraid, I would still go for it."

There were certain things that allowed Wilmer to keep going when he was on the brink of death, such as a great sense of gratitude and a burning desire not to die without achieving his goals.

"I didn't want my life to be ephemeral and fleeting," Wilmer told me. "I wanted, and I still want, my existence to have meaning, purpose, and to leave a legacy. Now I want to teach people that pain is inevitable, but suffering is optional."

According to Wilmer, this could be accomplished through self-awareness, meditation, and self-love. He fine-tuned the art of visualization, trusting wholeheartedly that we are capable of manifesting everything we visualize, feel, and work on. He believed that the repetition of affirma-tions regarding one's goals, combined with unshakeable conviction, can lead to achievements once thought impossible.

This is the process that allowed him to find Dr.

Cavadas—the man who made possible solutions that the doctors in Guatemala and the United States had said were impossible. The universe gave Wilmer people and circumstances one by one, year after year, to help him reach his ultimate goals.

"This makes me think that nothing is impossible. Sometimes we just still haven't figured out how to make it possible," Wilmer reflected with a grin.

So much of this perspective had come from Wilmer self-educating over the years. The spiritual awareness and maturity he'd gained came from a combination of life circumstances and mind-expanding books. After realizing the strength and perspective he gained from the books that guided his thoughts during the toughest moments of his life, Wilmer wanted to transfer that feeling of empowerment to others.

Before Wilmer left Jaime's house in Spain, he asked Jaime to reach out to all of his friends to donate books. He did just that, and the response was immediate and incredible. Wilmer traveled back to Guatemala with a suitcase filled with books to share with all the *pequeños* at NPH. His dream had begun, his heart was full, and his spirit was soaring.

6

MORE LIFE

On our fifth day of vacation, as our discussion in our family home in Washington over Thanksgiving break continued, I was reflecting on everything these two young men had shared with me during the prior four days. Wilmer was now twenty-nine, Jacinto twenty-eight, and both were flourishing in their lives and careers. Both were also filled with positive energy, ambition, and hope about the future.

Jacinto was continuing to take university classes in the business school while living and working in Guatemala City. He had a job working at AT&T in customer service. This was a high-level position in Guatemala for a university student, as it required workers to be completely fluent in multiple languages. He remained heavily involved at NPH and returned to the campus every week to visit, help out as needed, and spend time with Wilmer, who still lived in the clinic.

Jacinto was a year or two from graduating from business school and talked to me extensively about his plans for the future. He was excited to apply his business education in a real way and use his bilingual language skills to his advantage.

Jacinto and Wilmer were in the preliminary planning stages of opening a cafe in Antigua, Guatemala, whose proceeds would go toward supporting NPH. They wanted it to be a welcoming place filled with books, peace, and spiritual comfort. People could enjoy a warm cup of coffee or tea, choose a book from a wide selection, and support a good cause—all while meeting Jacinto and Wilmer and learning a bit about their story and the organization that raised them, if they happened to be working at the time. The brothers' plan was to provide work opportunities, not only for themselves in running the business, but for their NPH brothers and sisters (*hermanos mayores*) who wanted to work with them.

It was a beautiful plan, and I could tell how much joy the process of thinking through the details was bringing to Jacinto and Wilmer's lives.

In the time that I'd known Wilmer, I'd never seen him in such high spirits as he was during this trip. He was so full of life and excitement about the future. This was also the first time I'd ever seen him living without physical pain, and I could tell how much energy it brought him.

We took advantage of this opportunity. Jacinto had told my family at the beginning of this vacation that this trip was "all about Wilmer," because Jacinto had been in the area more often, and he wanted Wilmer to experience some of the same joys he'd had over the years. So between all our book discussions, we interspersed a wide variety of activities on Wilmer's "things I hope to do in Seattle" list. We took him to Snoqualmie Pass where he was surrounded by snow, made a snowball, and even tasted it. We drove to Lake Kachess, a favorite family vacation spot, where we sat along the shores and took in the serenity. We toured downtown Seattle where we bought fish from Pike Place Market, visited the gum wall, drank coffee at the first Starbucks, scaled the Space Needle, toured Microsoft, drank wine, ate good meals with lots of beef and shrimp (two of Wilmer's favorites), and shared in wonderful, rich conversations with friends and family as they came and went from our NPH Issaquah home. Wilmer also got to experience a true American Thanksgiving meal and help select a Christmas tree and decorate our home for the holidays. Our hearts were all full.

As we returned to the conversation about his life, Wilmer spoke excitedly about his studies. He was in business school and at the same time studying for his master's in digital marketing. He was also helping NPH with community outreach and partnerships, and taking English classes every Sunday. In his free time, he continued to devour books from a wide range of topics including business, neuroscience, economics, philosophy, and spirituality. He stood in such a strong place mentally, and it was uplifting to see his ambition skyrocketing and his pain levels almost nonexistent.

As he entered a new stage of his life where pain no longer determined his capabilities, the change was evident. Up until the surgeries in Spain, all of his introspective work, reading, and spiritual growth was applied towards conquering his own emotional and physical pain, and moving on with his own life. Now that the pain was out of the picture, he was able to redistribute all that knowledge, spirituality, and perspective into an actionable plan that would benefit himself and others. The internal goals that he'd worked so hard to attain were manifesting themselves into opportunity in the external world. I could feel his excitement and tell how important it was to him to be building something with his brother that incorporated everything they'd learned and gone through together.

One of Wilmer's primary goals at this stage in his life was to help others by telling his story. He wanted to be a sign of hope for people, to give them strength and drive while motivating them to make the most out of the lives they were given. He wanted to help people find what they were passionate about and gain the courage to chase after it relentlessly.

Wilmer had already started doing this on his own. He'd given speeches at several events, both in Guatemala and in the United States, in both English and Spanish. While visiting our family, he showed me the PowerPoint presentation he used when he gave these speeches, appropriately titled "Giving Up Is Not an Option." It was filled with slides that gave a snapshot rerun of his life—the hardships, the learning points, his philosophies, and quotes from some of the books he'd read.

There was no ego involved in the way Wilmer recalled the events of his life and told his story. His purpose in sharing wasn't for him, but for others. He saw himself and everything he had been through in life as a way to get people to think about their own lives and opportunities. He impacted people tremendously. He was already speaking at a variety of local events and giving motivational speeches for local companies at this point, but his dream was to travel the world as an ambassador for NPH while sharing his story and hopefully motivating people to become better versions of themselves.

This drive spurred Wilmer to ask me just prior to our visit that Thanksgiving, "Hey *hermano*, would you be interested in writing my life story?"

I was so humbled that he thought of me for this project, and I was grateful that he would entrust me with such an incredible opportunity. "Of course!! It would be an absolute honor and privilege," I assured him.

I spent multiple hours a day that first week in November of 2019 talking with Wilmer and Jacinto about their journey, the ups and downs, the progress, the road-blocks, and their ultimate vision for the future. Listening to them piece their story together in hindsight made it evident how much growth, learning, and struggle had accompanied them along the way. The bond they shared was something that had grown and matured over the years, from the turbulent waters of their upbringing to their current relationship as brothers and caretakers.

During their time in Washington, I asked about their relationship and the complications that came along with Wilmer's accident over the years. As much as Jacinto played the role of physical caretaker for Wilmer, when the emotional side became difficult, Wilmer stepped into his role as mental and spiritual caretaker for Jacinto—a role he'd become very familiar with throughout his life. I asked Jacinto if he ever felt pressure in his own life because of his own physical capabilities in comparison to Wilmer's.

"Not at first," Jacinto replied. But as Wilmer began to read more, become more emotionally intelligent, and visualize a better future for himself without complaining about his situation, that's when Jacinto started to feel pressure. "How can it be that he can't use his legs, and he is on his way to having a brighter future than me? I didn't know how to feel or react," Jacinto reflected, "but guess who helped me understand everything? Wilmer."

Wilmer helped Jacinto realize that *it's all in the mind* and *you attract what you think about.* Wilmer often recalled one of my mom's favorite quotes, "Where attention goes, energy flows, and neural pathways grow."

Jacinto said of his childhood, "I didn't read much. I

enjoyed hanging out with my friends and playing soccer in
my free time, so it was hard for me to understand this."
Jacinto continued, "So many people would compare me to
him, and ask, 'How can it be that he's this and you're that,
and you have so much more opportunity, etc.?' I felt enor-
mous pressure from this, and it was very hard on me. But
finally, with Wilmer's help, I understood it's not a competi-
tion. It's the opposite: we could help each other. Once I
understood that, we became an awesome team, and we
motivated each other every day."

"How does he motivate you?" I asked Jacinto.

"By the way he chooses to live his life—his hunger to
learn and help people. It's incredible to see how many
people go to him for advice, and he helps them with a big
smile on his face. He imagines a magnificent future for
himself; but he doesn't just wish for it, he works for it. He is
constantly reading; he's in university and getting his
masters all at once. He's so curious about things he doesn't
know and is constantly learning about things that interest
him.

"His smile is one of his best characteristics," Jacinto
reflected. "It's very rare to see him sad or angry. Wilmer
always tells me to read certain books and is always sending
me links to videos and important articles. I've learned so
much from his advice and recommendations. His desire to
help others motivates me a lot. He is learning to help
people and make a change in his community. He works for
NPH in public relations and is constantly forming new
partnerships with big companies and teaching them about
NPH Guatemala and the importance of helping the children and the underprivileged. Not only is he doing this at
NPH, but he has also done this in English in the United
States in front of hundreds of people. I am so proud of
him."

Jacinto continued, "Because of Wilmer, I know that things will happen that are unplanned and completely out of our control. There are people in much worse situations. That's always how life is, it could always be worse, so I try to be grateful for what I do have. His accident also brought us to NPH, which changed both of our lives for the better."

Reflections and Life Lessons

Seeing the level of peace and assurance that Wilmer had found in his life was motivating, especially after understanding where he'd come from and what he'd been through. Part of knowing the character that Wilmer possessed came from understanding how hard his life was, and consequently how much harder he had to work to get to a positive mental place.

Once he discovered and committed to his journey, Wilmer spent years sharpening and polishing his mind, taking on his problems head-on with an undeniable will to move closer to his goals.

Lying in bed one evening toward the end of Wilmer and Jacinto's visit, I couldn't help but reflect. Witnessing the way Wilmer chose to live and the courage he had made me want to become a better version of myself. I vowed that night to think of him on days when I felt unmotivated—to remember how he had to lie face down in a hospital bed for three months unable to move, but continued to read, listen to uplifting information, and repeat affirmations that kept his spirit alive and thriving. I thought about how frustrated he must have been for years watching his brother and friends go on living the way he wanted to…running, jumping, playing, being a part of a group as he watched from a distance in sadness. I wondered, *How deep did he have to dig to keep himself out of a dark place? What mentors did he have in that process? How unshakeable did his psyche have to be? How strong was his mind to move past all of that and find something, anything, that would give him the strength to carry on?*

He'd told me that all of that power—all of that acceptance and peace—came from a small rearrangement of his mind. "If you change the way you look at things, the things you look at will change," he'd say, quoting Wayne Dyer and Jack Sparrow in the same breath. "The problem is never the problem, your reaction to the problem is the problem."

In Wilmer's presence, it was impossible not to notice that he experienced much less independence than most people. If I wanted to walk down the stairs, I'd walk down the stairs. When I wanted to get out of bed, I'd get out of bed, go to the bathroom, shower, eat, and go where I wanted on my own time. No one was there to tell me when it was time to move on to the next activity, nor did anyone need to physically move me from one place to another. I could just do those things as I pleased. In my mind, these were freedoms I didn't necessarily feel lucky to experience, but when I saw Wilmer's level of dependence for all of these things, it reframed the way I thought about my own independence and physical capabilities.

Wilmer experienced almost zero personal freedoms, but when he discovered the power and control he could gain over his own mind, he was hooked. "I can be free in my mind," he would say. He could willingly choose to expose himself to books and information that would lift his spirits, challenge his mind, and ultimately teach him how to make his internal reality a place of happiness and peace.

When you cultivate an inner environment of peace, as Wilmer learned, your external reality begins to transform in that nature as well.

Wilmer realized through experience that when he had a negative attitude about his situation, that negativity reflected in his day-to-day external experience and his physical health. It wasn't until he paid close attention to his thoughts, and what he was feeding them, that he began to experience transformative change in his own happiness and interactions with other people.

Wilmer had been challenged so intensely throughout his life, mentally and physically, yet he still had a demeanor of peace and self-assurance that made people gravitate towards him. People felt those elements in his presence, and they wanted to know his secret.

The secret, as Wilmer shared, is the intentional ordering and upkeep of the mind. As Wilmer's favorite book, *Think and Grow Rich*, reaffirms, "Our brains become magnetized with the dominating thoughts which we hold in our minds, and by means with which no man is familiar, these 'magnets' attract us to the forces, the people, the circumstances of life which harmonize with the nature of our dominating thoughts."

Through experience and reading, Wilmer learned that we become magnets of our internal environment. Our subconscious mind is constantly gathering information and reaffirming what it's being fed. If we see the world through a negative lens, our subconscious mind will reaffirm that perspective and actively seek ways to harmonize with that in reality. Conversely, we can manipulate the way our brain works by deliberately filling the subconscious with positivity, spirituality, and love. Being aware of our thoughts—where they come from and where they go—is an important part of this process. Once we disassociate with that voice inside our head and realize that we actually have the power to control the dialogue, the world of potentiality will open up to us and begin to work in our favor.

Wilmer had a feeling of empowerment now that he was living pain-free. His life was beginning to bear the fruits of his labor. All those years spent in conscious effort to elevate his mind—all the books, lessons, struggles, and perspective changes—were now serving a larger purpose than just helping him cope with his pain. They were manifesting into opportunity—*real* opportunity. A path was opening up to him in a tangible way, and he was taking huge strides. I was excited to be on this journey with him.

7

TIMSHEL

While writing this book, there's a word I came across in a fiction book I was reading. The word was referenced in John Steinbeck's bestseller *East of Eden*, while the main character deals with questions of morality, free will, and good versus evil. The word is *timshel*, a Hebrew term that translates to *thou mayest*.

Timshel is also the word that God proclaimed to Cain while exiling him to the lands east of Eden after killing his brother Abel. He told Cain that he had the choice whether or not to overcome sin, and he chose not to.

The whole point is that as humans, we *can*…thou mayest.

I couldn't help but think of Wilmer when I reflected on this concept. No matter how dire his physical situation became, he believed he always had the choice of where to settle his mind. *There's always a choice*, I thought. God (or however you conceptualize divinity) gave man free will— the ability to decide, at every moment, the way they will see the world, and how they will behave. We are granted free will not only in small matters such as what to eat, what to wear, and who to be friends with, but also with larger, more polarized issues that weigh heavily on the human conscience. These are issues that make us choose between personal gain or doing what's right, living from a place of scarcity or abundance.

Wilmer made this connection when he discovered that he could make a conscious choice to live and experience a better life. His life wasn't summed up by his inability to walk. He could choose to stop focusing on what he *couldn't* do and shift it to the things he *could*, because *timshel*: *thou mayest.*

Wilmer told me there is serious power in the ability to change your mind—to stop the negative pattern-seeking that your brain will engage in if you let it. "I can decide right now to be happy," he'd say. "I can decide to have a good attitude about my problems. When this happens, the brain starts to work in a different way. It starts to look for better solutions to your problems." Everyone perceives themselves as having problems, but the response to these problems makes all the difference.

"Sometimes to change your attitude, all you need to do is think about something you're grateful for," Wilmer told me when I asked how he gets himself out of mental ruts. "When you send good energy to the universe, it comes back to you in some form. The universe functions just like we do. If you give someone a gift and they receive it with gratitude and good energy, you feel warmly about that person and will be more likely to want to give that person a gift again in the future or show more good energy toward them. The world constantly presents us with gifts. If we show gratitude for being a part of the world, it will continue to reward us. If you focus on the negative, it will be that."

Perhaps the greatest tragedy of our existence is that we

often forget that we have complete control over whether we will make the best of our experience, or the worst of it. The decision is always ours in the way we choose to think. If this concept isn't grasped, it's easy to end up living an entire lifetime in confusion and imitation instead of finding one's own meaning, identity, and purpose.

As a way to honor Wilmer, I'd like all the readers of his story to reflect on this question: *What is your own meaning?* Wilmer wanted to empower people by helping them understand that it's whatever you decide to make it. But it has to come from you. If you look outside for the answers, you'll quickly find yourself living someone else's life, thinking someone else's thoughts, and wasting precious time that could have been spent moving closer to your true source.

We're all in the same boat: confused and guessing. The difference is that some have fun with this ambiguity, and others view it as a personal hell they can't escape. No one has the answers, and there's no single, correct way to do anything, so you might as well give it your best shot and try to create some positivity and meaning for your own life. If you're unhappy with your life, chances are it has a lot to do with how you perceive the world and your life situation.

I can just hear Wilmer saying to all of us, "The good news is that it can be changed." You can reconsider which compass you let guide you through this world. If you follow society and see your life as a comparison to others, you might end up just like everybody else. If you follow your heart truly and choose gratitude, the world will open up to you.

You can put yourself in a position to be guided by your truest voice. It's impossible to successfully lie to yourself; your soul will know the truth, and it will suffer if you neglect that truth. But if you follow the truth, the soul rewards you with peace of mind, gratitude, understanding, and a humble excitement to *do what you should with what you have* at each moment. The choice is always yours, *timshel*.

Attitude Formula

Wilmer spoke to me in detail about Victor Kuppers's Attitude Formula. It's a simple equation that reads like this: $V=(K+S)A$. V stands for value, K for knowledge, S for skill, and A for attitude. The equation states that your potential output, through combining your knowledge and skills, will be compounded by the attitude you enter into it with.

Attitude is the thing that counts and makes people stand out in one direction or another. Skills and knowledge can be taught and learned, but the intangible difference-maker that is completely up to you is your attitude—how you choose to live and perceive the world—which ultimately makes the difference.

Kuppers believed that there aren't many losses that can truly justify losing your own joy. He believed there is a significant difference between going through a tragedy and having problems that last and linger.

Gratitude is the key, as is never letting your field of vision and attention focus solely on the things that didn't happen how you hoped they would. Attitude and perception are two things that only depend on you, and they can be powerful multipliers of life and happiness if used in the right way.

Wilmer took this equation to heart and used it as an example whenever sharing with people what helped him during his toughest days. Realizing that all the power and responsibility to change your life falls back on you, your state of mind, and your attitude can be either daunting or motivating. Wilmer chose to be motivated by this fact, recognizing it as an opportunity.

We may be able to shift our focus from something negative to something positive, but to live that way consistently takes serious work. It's hard not to be curious about the vehicle that Wilmer used to take his consciousness to that sacred and unshakable place he seemed to live in consistently. It's one thing to "live and learn and move forward," but when moving forward includes dealing with irreparable damage and pain every day for the rest of your life, the mind needs to work harder than it typically does to stay in a positive and progressive place.

Wilmer's accident forced him to make difficult decisions at a very young age. Everyone has hopes and dreams for their futures, with thoughts of who they want to become and what they'd like to do. But how do we react when those visions get pulled out from underneath us and completely destroyed? Wilmer not only had to choose to move forward, but to do so with positivity, humility, and an open mind every single day, in a world that looked massively different than what he had originally imagined for himself.

Meditation

At one point during our conversation in 2019, I asked him directly, "What keeps you going during the hard days?"

He looked me in the eye and said, "Good strong coffee, red wine…" he paused, "ah, and meditation," he said with a grin.

I laughed because I genuinely thought he was kidding.

"No, for real!" he said with conviction.

At that time, I had tried meditation once or twice before, but I'd never made an effort to turn it into any sort of legitimate practice. I thought it was for people who couldn't sit still. Wilmer could *only* sit still, which is why I was so confused that he would want to do so even more intentionally than he was already forced to.

I had a lot to learn about the power of meditation. Wilmer helped me realize that meditation can be the tool that helps you develop control over your mind and thoughts, which ultimately decides the type of life you live.

If the mind is the ultimate decider of the type of life we'll live, meditation is the practice that allows us to tune into how the mind really works. Our brains are pattern-seeking mechanisms. That's how we identify things in our physical world. Everything has a name; everything has a reason. From just after the time we can walk, we begin school to learn how to learn.

Conventional, linear knowledge is thrown at us for eighteen years with certain parameters about what's right and what's wrong. Yet there was never really any structure or system put in place to teach us what's actually going on in our minds as we learn—how it identifies patterns, reaffirms what it has already been exposed to, and then jumps to a conclusion. This is why when you see a tree, you think "tree" in your mind. You don't think about the physical qualities and particles of matter and energy that make the thing what it is. It's just a tree.

The problem is that we fall into this same way of thinking when it comes to how we think about ourselves. Our identities are often formed from the way we've thought about ourselves for years: *I'm not smart enough*, or *I'm ugly*, or *I'm not creative*.

We also perceive ourselves in the context of others. What have other people said about us for our whole lives? Is that a reflection of us or them? Is the way we see ourselves the truth? Or have we just heard it enough times in our thoughts to believe it? Can we change the dialogue?

Wilmer would say *yes*. He helped me learn that the process of observing our own thoughts through meditation is a sort of mental superpower when used the right way. As Wilmer learned from the books *Think and Grow Rich* and *The Power of Now*, our lives will harmonize with the dominating thoughts we let enter our minds.

Meditation creates a portal for you to observe what these thoughts are. It also exposes you to your power to either accept or deny thoughts as they come up. Allowing some thoughts to pass and others to resonate is where the freedom and growth begins.

Sitting in meditation allows you to understand how fleeting and random a thought can be. They fade away as quickly as they arise, if we let them. Our brains, being the pattern-seekers that they are, fixate on the thoughts we deem important or the thoughts our minds are exposed to the most. Therefore, your life will be the result of whatever you expose your mind to the most. Meditation is the vehicle that helps you understand this, but the growth happens in the application of this principle in your everyday life.

Your subconscious mind is always picking up cues from your environment. The mind is always on. You might think of yourself as a pretty positive person, but there's value in developing the skills to remain that way when something goes sideways in your life. Exercising the body every day is normal. Exercising the mind every day is just as valuable, but less normal in our Western society.

The average American spends close to four hours watching TV every day, and another two to three hours engaged on social media. That is a huge chunk of the day

It's entertaining but also potentially dangerous to our mental state.

Social media has created a comparison culture among people in our society that leaves many feeling inadequate any time they open up their phones. The news and other TV stations search for stories with captivating headlines that will draw a reaction out of its audience. Whether it's truthful or not, viewership is the priority. This typically leads to news stories that instigate fear or hatred and TV shows or movies that take a deep dive into murder and crime or glorify war and violence. With these being the central themes of the media we intake, it's a little frightening to think that the average person is spending six to seven hours consuming every day—and that's only the six to seven hours of active time. The rest of the day, the subconscious mind is replaying these themes and creating a filter that ultimately flows up to our perspective of the world and our own life.

There is magic in understanding this concept that the mind is always on, always taking in new information and digesting it to create new ideas and new realities in our world. If we take a nonchalant approach to this idea, we will be puppeteered by our minds and identify with anything it tells us without questioning the source. However, once this concept is grasped, we can begin the process of mastering our minds.

Wilmer did this, and that's what allowed him to survive some of the toughest moments in his life. His mind became a safe haven from all the external negativity and doubt that followed him. He wouldn't contribute to that negativity; there was quite enough of it as it was. When there was nothing to be positive about, he worked hard to find the lesson that the struggle could teach him.

As discussed in this chapter, Wilmer learned that the

brain seeks out patterns and reaffirms anything that it's being fed repeatedly. When the doctors in Chicago told him that his operation was impossible and that they wouldn't take it on, it would have been easy for him to believe that narrative. He'd heard professional opinions from people who had spent their entire lives studying and practicing medicine. What did he know compared to them? He could have let his mind travel down that pathway of hopelessness, but that wasn't Wilmer's style. What kept his mind in a positive state throughout that experience was his ability to remain focused on his goals. At that point, it was a singular goal: find a solution to stay alive.

It was the belief that he *could* that ultimately led Wilmer to Dr. Cavadas and the surgery that saved his life in Spain. Without this intense conviction that there had to be a solution, Wilmer would have left Chicago completely deflated, returning to Guatemala to live out the short remainder of his life.

Wilmer taught me that we always have two options: to throw in the towel, or continue to fight. You are the only one who can truly pull the plug on your own beliefs, and Wilmer wasn't ready to do that yet.

Mind Games

Wilmer didn't have anyone in his personal circle who could fully understand what he was going through. Since he didn't have a mentor guiding him through this experience, he found help through books, lectures, and the internet, as we've explored. He understood the power of the subconscious mind and figured out that the more time he spent intentionally consuming content that would create feelings of positivity within himself, the more those feelings would transmute into his external life. He trained his brain to actively seek out positivity by consistently exposing himself to its sources in his downtime.

One person who Wilmer drew tremendous strength from was a man named Nick Vujicic. Nick was born with a rare condition called tetra-amelia, born without arms and legs. He wrote a book called *Life Without Limits*, which made a tremendous impact on Wilmer. Although they never met, I know Wilmer considered Nick to be a role model and mentor, someone whose words he could lean on for motivation during hard times. The premise of Nick's book and life philosophy is that living from a place of gratitude for what you do have, rather than thinking about what you don't, will create a fulfilling life. Here are some of the quotations from Nick's book that were underlined in the copy that Wilmer kept with him:

- *"In life you have a choice: Bitter or Better? Choose better, forget bitter."*
- *"I never met a bitter person who was thankful. Or a thankful person who was bitter."*
- *"I encourage you to accept that you may not be able to see a path right now, but that doesn't mean it's not there."*
- *"Don't put your life on hold so that you can dwell on the unfairness of past hurts."*
- *"Yet I also believe that when you do unto others, blessings come to you as well. So if you don't have a friend, be a friend. If you are having a bad day, make someone else's day. If your feelings are hurt, heal those of another."*
- *"If you can't get a miracle, become one"* (Vujicic 2010).

Wilmer told me that Vujicic had even learned how to surf. A man with no arms and no legs learned how to surf in the ocean! He looked at me, knowing that I'd been living in California for the last five years, and asked with a chuckle, "Do you even know how to surf?" I didn't, but I started learning later that year, with Wilmer and Vujicic as my motivation.

The point is, Wilmer didn't *have* to do any of this. He didn't have to devour self-help books, watch compelling seminars, study the complexities of the mind, and become curious about practically anything he could learn about. But he did. He chose to, and that's what ultimately made the difference and allowed him to live a happy and fulfilled life.

Reading connected Wilmer with wisdom from people who had championed their own lives despite serious setbacks. These were people who were curious. They thought and acted differently, challenged the norms of society, and encouraged others to do the same. Learning from them allowed Wilmer to feel a sense of community and live his life on the shoulders of those he considered giants. He took everything to heart, and it was reflected in his everyday encounters and actions, and felt in his presence.

8

GOALS

On one of the last days Wilmer and Jacinto were in Washington, I took them to Microsoft where we met a friend of mine, Michael, who gave the boys a full tour of the campus and treated them to lunch in the cafeteria (which looked more like the food court of a gigantic mall). He walked us through all the different departments and showed us new technologies and gadgets the different teams were working on. Wilmer and Jacinto both tried out the virtual reality race-car-driving simulator (which didn't perform well). They also stood in front of the digital camera screen that took a mapping of their faces and guessed how old they were. They probably went in five times each, giggling with one another as the screen guessed ages based on the goofy faces they were making for the camera. Their childlike playfulness felt contagious.

Wilmer and Jacinto both had a decent grasp of the tech world, but they'd never experienced anything like this. I could tell it was fascinating to them. When Michael gave us an insight into how many different people around the world were working for the Microsoft team, I could see a

lightbulb go off in Wilmer's head as he realized how technology could truly make communication, opportunity, and
connection possible for people like him and Jacinto.

We passed by a team that was working on graphic
design for a new game. The characters were fantastical and
imaginative, essentially looking like the grown-up version
of a childhood sketchbook filled with drawings of action
figures. The employees seemed to be having fun, and I
noticed Wilmer studying the work they were doing with a
keen interest.

"Thinking about giving your drawing skills a go?" I
asked him sarcastically, but he was lost in thought.

When we sat down for lunch, Wilmer looked at
Michael and asked the somewhat rhetorical question, "So
that's a *job*? Those people back there who were sketching
drawings on the computer, that's what they do?" He was
blown away. In the world Jacinto and Wilmer grew up in,
jobs were practical rather than imaginative. Kids around
him weren't raised to believe that their unique artistic abilities could turn into career opportunities. They were raised
knowing that labor or service jobs waited for them in the
future. Creativity was rarely discussed as a means to make
money. Because of this, talented, artistic kids had no outlet
except their sketchbooks for their imaginative pursuits to
turn into anything.

"Can you imagine if Oliver knew this was a job?"
Wilmer asked Jacinto with excitement. Oliver was a friend
of theirs who grew up with them at NPH. He was a kid
who, like many others there, spent his downtime drawing,
sketching, painting, and creating, with no real concept that
it was an admirable talent that companies would pay
employees thousands of dollars a year to do in a more
targeted and developed way.

"If the kids at NPH knew this was an option, it would

change everything," Wilmer said. "It would give them hope, something to look forward to and strive for, something that would expand their world and give them a chance to support themselves and their families in a different way. Right now, many children at NPH think they are destined for physical labor jobs when they grow up. Farming, woodworking, trade jobs that employ the body more than the mind. Having access to opportunities like this would change everything for our creative brothers and sisters…and they don't even know it exists!"

When we got back to my house, Wilmer was electric. He immediately got on his laptop to message his friends about the day. He was filled with energy and vigorously typed his new ideas as quickly as he could get them out. It was important to him to involve NPH and the *pequeños* there in his future plans. He wanted to build his future in a way that would allow him to use his network and life experiences to provide opportunity for others and encourage them to chase after their own dreams.

Wilmer's world had been massively expanded because of his life circumstances. He'd traveled and become exposed to new people, places, and things. This motivated him and filled him with new ideas for his own life. He realized how much perspective he'd gained from these experiences and felt compelled to share his discoveries with his NPH brothers and sisters to help create hopefulness and excitement about their futures.

Wilmer and Jacinto were set to return to Guatemala in two days. This amazing holiday season at our home was coming to an end too quickly. Wilmer wanted to spend his last full day brainstorming, organizing, and planning out both the structure of the book, and an updated business model for his coffee shop and wellness center with Jacinto. So that's what we did.

The following day I sat with Wilmer, Jacinto, and my girlfriend Tori in my family's dining room for the last time. We had just spent four to six hours per day over the last ten days recording the detailed description of their childhoods, the accident, going to NPH for the first time, finding opportunity, and how Wilmer and Jacinto's relationship as brothers evolved over the years. They told me about their dreams and goals for the future and how they planned to take their business plan from concept to reality once they graduated from school. Their aspirations were big, and both shared how important it was that their experience be shared. Whatever the future held, they believed they were better suited to take it on together.

We ended that day with a plan. The next day when we took Wilmer and Jacinto to the airport, it would not be goodbye for long. One month later, Tori and I were set to meet them in Guatemala to spend a month doing more research and beginning writing the story of Wilmer's life.

9

GUATEMALA

That following month went by quickly, and before I knew it, Tori and I were days away from our departure for Guatemala. I'd spent the weeks leading up to our trip reaching out to people from Wilmer's past who I hoped to connect with once I got there—people who knew Wilmer at different stages in his life and could help me shape his story. The response I received from everyone I reached out to served as a testament to the impact Wilmer had made on people throughout his life. Without fail, each person responded with a resounding *yes*, letting me know they were willing and excited to help in any way possible.

We rented an Airbnb in a town called Antigua that was about a fifteen-minute bus ride from NPH. Antigua, with its cobblestone streets and colorful buildings, is a beautiful city that lies at the base of three volcanoes—Agua, Acatenango, and Fuego. The whole city is walkable, and travelers from all over the world frequent the bars, hostels, shops, and restaurants daily. In a single night out, it's not uncommon to meet people from seven or eight different countries—all passing through to carry on with their travels in Central and South America.

The plan was to spend my days writing and gathering bits and pieces of Wilmer's story from the people who knew him best. I'd arranged several meetings with people who knew Wilmer at different stages of his life: friends, nurses, teachers, etc. I would do my interviews in the morning and write in the afternoons and evenings.

On the third day, I went to NPH to visit Wilmer and talk to him more about the book. I met him in his room at the clinic, the room in which he'd spent the majority of his life. The walls were filled with photos from his life, postcards from his travels, and notes from friends and loved ones. A large bookshelf next to his desk was filled with mind-expanding books on topics ranging from meditation and neuroscience, to economics and business.

He was neatly folding some clothes and humming to himself when I walked in, and when he saw me, he greeted me with his signature ear-to-ear grin and an overexaggerated "heyyy BRO." He loved saying the word *bro*, and it was always a little hilarious hearing him use it with his terrible American accent.

Wilmer's smile filled up the room, and I immediately felt a sense of warmth being in his presence. *It shouldn't be rare to feel like someone's really with you when you're in their presence*, I thought. I considered how attention was usually split, and it wasn't uncommon for people to answer texts or scroll Instagram while talking with them. *When you're with Wilmer, you have his full attention. He thinks deeply about everything you say, and he listens thoroughly before responding.*

We joked around for a few minutes before heading to the cafeteria. On the brief walk over, Wilmer greeted everyone we encountered with the same gigantic smile. He seemed to have a personalized inside joke with each person we passed. When we made it to the cafeteria, he ordered us coffees at the counter as I found a table. I set up a camera to record our conversation, and he joked about making sure it was facing his "good side." I told him every side was his good side, and he smirked and said, "I know."

After we finished our interview, a younger boy from NPH approached Wilmer with an admiring smile. The boy was probably twelve years old, and he used a walker. It was clear he didn't have full function in his legs, and I could tell by the way they interacted that Wilmer was a huge role model to this boy. *Another example of the strength Wilmer gives to others by simply being himself,* I told myself.

Tori and I spent a memorable month in Guatemala, and as our departure day approached, I felt closer to Wilmer than I ever had in my life. We spent long days together going over every detail of his life and journey. Time flew with him. He was incredibly captivating and had a nonchalant way of delivering profound wisdom to every conversation. Through collecting his story, I gained a new perspective on my own life that I would carry with me forever.

We left Guatemala in February of 2020. On our last night there, we went to Yecenia's house for dinner and a small get-together. Wilmer and Jacinto were both there, along with several of their friends and the six dogs that lived in the house. Everyone was drinking and having a good time as we reminisced on the last month spent there.

I was sad to be leaving, but spirits were high. We'd created a lot of momentum in that month, and we had a lot of exciting things to look forward to. I'd made some serious progress on the book by collecting Wilmer's story from the people in his life, and Wilmer was working hard writing out his answers to many of the deeper questions I'd presented him with.

We set a schedule to remain in contact to work on the book and create a business plan for how to market it. Wilmer was working on a website to promote it, and we were both trying to think of a name that would do the story justice.

On that last night, Wilmer was more reserved than I was used to seeing him. He was quiet and kept mostly to himself as everyone else enjoyed the party and socialized with one another. I looked over at him several times and thought how tough it must be for him at times when he recognized his limitations.

For most of us, if we're not enjoying a party or a social gathering, we could simply call ourselves an Uber, sneak out unannounced, and sleep it off. For Wilmer, no process was ever that simple. If he wanted to leave, he'd need to get help from his brother or friends to carry him out of the house and into a car. He'd then have to make sure the Uber driver was willing to help him out of the car and back into his wheelchair upon arrival. Then, a worker at NPH would have to push him up the hill and help him into his bed at the clinic.

Seeing him in those moments of quiet frustration made me think about the freedoms I often took for granted.

I reflected on how Wilmer had spent his whole life intentionally seeking out the silver lining of every situation, but no one could do that all the time. *Sometimes the darkness, sadness, and grief wins, and negativity rises to the surface even amidst conscious efforts to fight it down.* I imagined this was the case for Wilmer at times.

I leaned down to give him a hug in his wheelchair as we were preparing to leave. I thanked him for a wonderful month spent together and told him we had a lot to look forward to, and a lot of work to do. I left saying I would see him soon.

I didn't know it at the time, but that night was the last time I would ever see Wilmer alive.

10

LOCKDOWN

COVID-19 made its way onto the scene shortly after my return to the United States. People began to stock up on toilet paper and canned goods, preparing for the apocalypse, while others speculated that it would blow over in two weeks at most.

Wilmer was back at NPH and had returned to his busy schedule of school and work. Jacinto was living in the city at the time, and before anyone could grasp the gravity of the situation, there was word about mandated lockdowns and quarantine. The Guatemalan government issued a nationwide 4:00 p.m. to 4:00 a.m. curfew and prohibited citizens from traveling outside of the zone they lived in. Since NPH is in a different zone than where Jacinto lived in the city, the brothers wouldn't be able to see each other until the mandates were lifted.

Wilmer had been living pain-free since his surgery in Spain. The ulcer had healed, and he hadn't experienced any complications with his reconstructed spine. But in early March of 2020, just as COVID restrictions were increasing, Wilmer began to notice a twinge of pain stemming from the area in his back where the ulcer had been.

The nurses at the NPH clinic gave Wilmer antibiotics to manage the pain and stop any infections from spreading. They were tentative to bring him into any hospitals, as COVID was running rampant and no one knew the full implications of the virus. Hospital beds were taken up by COVID patients, and he'd run the risk of exposing himself by even being on the premises.

The antibiotics didn't seem to help, and Wilmer's pain increased by the day. The skin covering the place where the ulcer had been started to crack and open again. Jacinto was mostly unaware of the pain Wilmer was experiencing, because in classic Wilmer form, when they caught up on the phone, he never shared the hardships he was going through. Jacinto was living in Guatemala City at the time, which is about an hour away from NPH where Wilmer was living. Because of the COVID lockdowns, they could only communicate over the phone.

The pain reached a point of being unbearable for Wilmer. He begged the clinic workers to take him to a hospital in the city to see what was going on. They eventually did. The hospital took x-rays and ran tests, and found that a screw from the surgery in Spain had come loose.

The doctor told Wilmer that it was likely the screw coming loose which started the pain. It was now July, and Wilmer had been feeling pain since March. They were forced to perform immediate surgery to reposition the screw and fight back the infections and other destruction it had caused.

Keep in mind that Wilmer's previous surgery was the first ever of its kind—risky, highly unique, and requiring certain levels of experimentation and creativity to pull off. And the life-saving surgery had been performed by Dr.

Cavadas in Spain. Wilmer was now being worked on by a doctor who was seeing his situation for the first time, in a hospital that was overflowing from patients with COVID. Wilmer's condition was severe again. Dr. Cavadas wanted to come to Guatemala to help but was unable to given the country's lockdown restrictions.

The local doctor did what he could to reset the screw and cover the wound that had opened back up. Jacinto wasn't allowed to see his brother at the hospital as he recovered. They weren't allowing visitors because of the pandemic.

When Wilmer was awake and coherent, he called Jacinto. Expecting a status update from Wilmer, Jacinto answered eagerly.

"Can you order me some Chinese food to the hospital?" Wilmer's weak voice asked through the phone.

Jacinto, laughing incredulously, made it happen.

Letting Go

After a few more days spent in recovery in the hospital, Wilmer returned to NPH. His health required constant attention from the clinic workers. He had fallen behind in his classes and had to make the decision to take a break from school for the upcoming semester. His health was the main priority, and with a pandemic sweeping the globe, his already weakened immune system was at constant risk, not only for COVID, but for reinfection.

About two weeks after returning to NPH, in mid-August, Wilmer's pain returned. He began to lose weight rapidly and was suffering repetitive cycles of fevers and chills.

Over the years, Wilmer's body had been weakened by

all the operations and changes he had experienced physically.

My mom remembers multiple phone conversations with Jacinto during the last three months of Wilmer's life. She said Jacinto was quite frustrated that he couldn't visit Wilmer at NPH due to the lockdown. She, too, was struggling.

Several of Wilmer's internal organs were losing function and shutting down. He was as weak as he'd ever been, and as small as he had ever been. At this time, Wilmer weighed only seventy pounds, which was thirty pounds lighter than his normal weight.

"If you don't get down here, you're never going to see your brother alive again." Yecenia's voice came over the phone in a frantic call to Jacinto. Jacinto hadn't seen his brother in six months because of the COVID mandates. Yecenia, fortunately during that time, was in constant contact with Wilmer as she worked at NPH and would stop in the clinic daily to check on him prior to his return to the hospital.

Jacinto found a way to get down to NPH and was shocked by the appearance of his brother. "His arm was like this," he would later say to me and choke up, forming a tiny circle with his thumb and pointer finger. Wilmer had essentially deteriorated into a shell of himself during the time that had passed since Jacinto saw him last. Wilmer had always been small, but now it looked like he wasn't even there.

Wilmer looked and felt horrible, but he still found the strength to joke around with his brother. He'd been fighting for his life since he was nine years old. Every day was a physical and mental struggle in one way or another. For twenty years he'd been fighting, overcoming pain.

"Keep fighting, keep fighting Wilmer, keep fighting."

"I know you have it in you, if anyone can overcome this it's you, Wilmer."

"Dig deep, you can do this."

These were words he had heard over and over again, for twenty years. *Keep fighting.*

And every time, Wilmer found his way back. That's what made it so difficult to believe or accept that this time might be different.

"It's OK," Jacinto told him instead. "Whatever you want, it's OK. I'll be right here for you."

Jacinto knew that Wilmer had so much love in his heart —and courage to keep fighting until his last breath, even when everything in his body was screaming for him to let go. Wilmer had lived his entire life on the brink of letting go. Jacinto, in a final act of brotherhood and love, was giving him permission to finally do so. Jacinto wanted Wilmer to know that he didn't have to keep fighting. He wanted his brother to accept that if he wanted to let go, it would be OK—whatever he wanted. He didn't want him to suffer anymore. That took tremendous strength, strength that I wouldn't have possessed in that situation.

We often want people to stay here, to stay on this earth for our sake, because it makes us happy to have them around. We don't always think about how they are feeling.

Jacinto considered Wilmer's feelings, not his own, in giving him permission to let go. "You don't have to keep fighting, Wilmer," Jacinto reassured his brother. "It's time for you to know peace."

Wilmer became so weak that they had no choice but to bring him back to a hospital. Jacinto checked him into Hospital La Paz in the city, where doctors took his vitals and ran tests to determine the severity of his immediate condition. His body was failing. He needed nutrients yet had no appetite because of the pain he was experiencing internally. The doctors resorted to feeding him through a tube while pumping him full of antibiotics and monitoring his heartbeat through the night.

He spent the next day drifting in and out of consciousness. The doctor met with Jacinto, Yecenia, and the national director and director of family services at the NPH home to discuss financing Wilmer's hospital stay and treatment. The reality was that Wilmer needed another large operation to correct what was going wrong. The problem was that Wilmer was too thin, and his body was too weak to survive an operation of that magnitude. In order to survive, he needed a surgery that would kill him.

Wilmer woke up later that evening with a burst of energy. He called Jacinto with a single focus: he wanted Chinese food again. Jacinto found a way to get into the hospital to see Wilmer and bring him his order. It was during this visit that Jacinto called my mom and gave her the opportunity to talk with Wilmer.

She recalls asking Wilmer if there was anything he needed to feel more comfortable in the hospital. "As a mom, I was desperate to get him whatever he needed, because I couldn't be there for him in person," she told me. "But true to Wilmer's form, he said, 'Thank you, Cathy, but I am fine. Don't worry about me. They are taking good care of me here.' He spoke with such deep humility and grace, in the beautiful voice I had come to know and cherish, and all in English."

She added, "A short time later, Jacinto found a way to call me one last time, just days before Wilmer's passing. As hard as the prior phone call was, this one was much more difficult. On this day, Wilmer barely had the energy to speak. His voice was so weak it came out as a whisper, and only Spanish words were spoken, which was a true sign of his complete and utter exhaustion. I knew then that this would be my last time speaking to him. I was utterly devastated. It took everything I had to compose myself, and in that moment, I let him know how much I loved him. I thanked him for his life and everything he gave to me and my entire family, and everyone he'd ever met. I promised him that he would not be forgotten and that I would find a way to keep his dreams alive."

After making relative progress from the condition that had brought him into the hospital, Wilmer then contracted a fever and was moved to the ICU on Friday, August 28, 2020, two days before Jacinto's twenty-ninth birthday. He could no longer regulate oxygen or breathe on his own, and he was being kept alive by a breathing machine.

At this time, the hospital was allowing only one sibling at a time to be with Wilmer. Seeing him in person in this state was extremely difficult. Jacinto was struck by the image of his unconscious brother in the ICU, breathing through a tube in his throat. Standing alongside his bed, Jacinto spoke to Wilmer, saying, "I'm not going to tell you everything's going to be alright, or to fight for your life, or to fight for us. It's whatever you want...I'm right here… whatever you want."

The doctor then approached Jacinto and told him that both of Wilmer's kidneys were failing. He confirmed again that his body was not healthy enough to survive surgery. He told Jacinto to prepare for the worst, and that Wilmer could be dead in a matter of hours.

11

THE FINAL GOODBYE

On August 30, 2020, Wilmer Arias passed away in the hospital. It was 2:00 a.m., two hours into Jacinto's birthday, when he received the call. Jacinto sat in his bed, shocked and numb. For as many close calls that Wilmer had lived through, this was finally it. Wilmer was really gone.

Jacinto called my mom immediately after he found out. That conversation is etched in stone in my mom's memory.

"I woke up to a phone call in the middle of the night," she recalled to me. "As soon as I heard Jacinto's voice, I knew Wilmer had passed. We sat on the phone for a while, crying together from a distance. I hated that I couldn't be with Jacinto in this moment. I would have given anything to reach through that phone line to touch his face and hold him, like any mother would hold their child when they're in such excruciating pain. I was so full of conflicting emotions. I was utterly devastated, yet grateful that Wilmer was no longer suffering. I was angry that the world took another beautiful soul from us, when what this world truly needs is more Wilmers. I knew in that moment there were no words that could be said to comfort Jacinto...so we sat in the silence for a few minutes, both holding on to our phones, neither one of us wanting to hang up. But eventually, Jacinto had to go. There were more phone calls to be made, and things to be done."

Jacinto sat up the rest of the night, waiting a few more hours to call his sister, Yecenia. He wanted to give her a few more hours of rest before waking her, as he knew how difficult this news was going to be for her.

When Jacinto called her in the morning to tell her the news, she went into shock and began hyperventilating so intensely that Jacinto thought he might lose two siblings that day. Her grief took over her body, giving her violent convulsions. Wilmer had been her rock. He had kept her positive and taught her how to direct her mindset to a happy destination. She and Wilmer had spent hours together daily. She'd helped him with his activities while Jacinto was in the city.

Amidst the struggle—amidst the obstacles, the loss, the pain—the siblings always had each other's backs. Against terrible odds, they had navigated their way to a better life together as a family.

They say difficult circumstances bring people closer together. When you lose those people, the resilience you've built with them and through them can all come crashing down, leaving a hollow void in your soul that was once filled with their presence. This is a void that will soon be filled by their memory, but until then, all you get is the void —the sinister pit that sits in your stomach and throat, threatening to send you manic at any moment.

My mom had been keeping my family updated on Wilmer's condition after her phone calls, as we knew it would be difficult for Jacinto to connect with all of us. I sat quietly in my room after I heard the news, not sure how to process the information. I felt sadness and relief at the same time. I knew Wilmer had been suffering greatly for months. I felt relieved that he was at peace, but a deep sadness overcame me as I realized how big of a hole would be left without Wilmer's presence on earth.

"I don't know why, but I had a really hard time going in to look at the body," Jacinto later told me. "I asked the doctor if he could be in the room with us while we saw him. I couldn't do it alone."

Seeing such a beautiful and vibrant soul reduced to a shriveled, lifeless body felt wrong to Jacinto. Wilmer was so much bigger than his physical appearance. He was a giant. To Jacinto, he'd represented a feeling. The security of knowing that Wilmer was there in the world gave Jacinto confidence, perspective, security, and bravery his entire life. When they were in it together, nothing ever felt too bad or unbearable. They knew they had each other to lean on, and that was always enough.

This emotion—the feeling that you have someone in the world who really knows and understands you—creates a full life and identity of its own, a security in yourself that exists because of the shared experience you've had with another. How do you replace that? You can't.

"It's not about moving on," Jacinto reminded me. "It's about moving forward."

12

DEAR WILMER

After Wilmer's death, I struggled to move on. It was hard to believe he was gone when his life had been so full. Following is a letter I wrote, after some time had passed, to express how I felt and what his life meant to me. I plan to keep it with me forever.

I shared this letter at Wilmer's celebration of life that we organized in our home parish, St. Louise. Because of COVID, the service wasn't open to the public, but my family gathered with a closeknit group of our extended NPH family, and we live streamed it to all of Wilmer's family and friends from around the world who wanted to join us in this celebration of a life well-lived.

Dear Wilmer,

When I heard that you had passed away, my heart sank into my stomach, and my body experienced the typical numbness that comes along with deep sadness. I sat quietly in my room, processing the information and reminiscing on the last time I had seen and spoken to you.

Something urged me to get up and go outside for a walk. I know that you were with me on this walk, because my feelings of sadness suddenly began to transform into deep gratitude, and an overwhelming feeling of love and connectedness to my surroundings and the people I encountered.

Last November, you and I began a project together to document your life story and learnings. In the process, I spent hours interviewing you, becoming more fascinated with your character and perspective of the world during each session. One of your answers in particular came to mind that Sunday when I went out for a walk.

In our conversations, I asked you what you think happens to us when we die.

This is what you told me. . . .

"If I have learned anything in my life, it's that what is important is how you choose to live, here and now. It doesn't matter what happens when we die; we won't know until we get there. What matters is that we live harmoniously without ego or selfishness, that we live the best we can and strive to find our purpose in life. If you're happy with who you are and what you're doing and live with spiritual abundance, you will have found your purpose. You will leave a legacy that inspires the people around you to find that same level of peace, spirituality, and purpose that you were able to find."

Wilmer, you certainly left a legacy. Thinking of you as I walked that day, I noticed I wanted to smile more. I wanted to say hello to people, breathe deeply, laugh, appreciate my life, reach out to loved ones, and be a better person for myself and others. As these feelings rushed over me, I felt your presence in everything I looked at. I felt your spirit in the breeze, your playfulness and sense of humor in the squirrels and birds, and your strength in the trees.

I don't believe that you feared death. You seemed to have a spiritual awareness inside of you that knew wherever you were going was OK—that it would make you even more a part of the larger universal consciousness that flows through all of us. You used to tell me that you believed heaven and hell are both just states of mind, and we have the ability to choose where we want to be every second of every day based on our mindset, attitude, and decisions.

You played a spiritual role in many people's lives. You were a constant reminder to people that life could be good amidst any circumstances. You would say, "The problem is not the problem, your reaction to the problem is the problem," with a beaming I know this is true; you can't argue with me smile on your face.

You fought so hard your entire life to find this level of peace, consciousness, and control over your mind, and something that was important to you was sharing this ability with others. You were on a path to enlightenment, and you wanted everyone to come with you.

So Wilmer, it broke my heart that you had to leave us so soon. There was so much left to do. But today I challenge myself to take a lesson out of your playbook: "When you change the way you look at things, the things you look at change." A tragedy, yes. But also an opportunity. An opportu-

nity to live intentionally with your memory. To think deeply, seek out positivity at all costs, feed my mind with uplifting information, empower others, and spread peace with kind words and actions.

Wilmer, you will remain my teacher, my spiritual guide, and my inspiration as I continue on with my life. Your memory and the wisdom you shared with me and others will serve as a constant reminder to live well, and live now. I can picture you now, laughing and smiling, with a big cup of coffee in between your two palms—pain-free, and looking down on us with love.

I have cried for you, Wilmer, and I miss you deeply. But today I feel like smiling, and that's how I know you're here.

Cuidate hermano, y te veré en la próxima vida. (Take care my brother, and I will see you in the next life.)

JOIN THE NPH FAMILY

To be a part of NPH means to become a member of an extended family that helps to transform the lives of thousands of children and families throughout Latin America and the Caribbean. With the help of others from around the world, you will provide homes, health care services, and educational programs in a safe and loving environment—giving children the best chance for success to become leaders in their own communities.

Wilmer's life was just one example of how NPH creates life-changing opportunities for disadvantaged and vulnerable children and youth living in extreme conditions. Through a comprehensive approach that embraces the whole child, NPH supports children to become independent, caring adults who give back to their communities—shaping better futures for themselves, their families, and their world.

Breaking generational poverty begins with helping one child at a time. Consider sponsoring a child or university student, volunteering locally or internationally, or supporting a community program or special project, and you too can witness firsthand the impact of your support.

Please help keep Wilmer's dreams alive and become a part of the NPH family by visiting www.nphusa.org or www.nph.org (outside of the USA), and match your gifts with the needs of our NPH family.

NOTE FROM BISHOP RON HICKS

In 1954, Father William Wasson founded NPH in Mexico as a place to care for and raise orphaned, abandoned, and at-risk children. He wanted to create a place different from other institutions or NGOs. His heart's desire was to create a family with unconditional love at its core.

Since that time, NPH has grown to nine homes in Latin America and the Caribbean and expanded to care for vulnerable and needy children living outside the NPH homes. What has remained steadfast throughout the years is that NPH transforms the lives of everyone it touches, including the children, the volunteers (like Matthew who wrote this book), the staff, and the donors. Once someone joins the NPH family, there is a bond that continues forever!

After graduating from college in 1989, I volunteered for one year at NPH Mexico. During that year, I not only learned Spanish, but discerned a call to enter the Major Seminary. Answering that call led me to being ordained a priest in 1994 and a Bishop in 2018. Because of this providential detour to NPH, my life changed for the better. I thank God for my continued connection to this amazing family.

In 2005, I started a five-year assignment as the regional director of NPH Central America. While living at NPH El Salvador, I would frequently visit the NPH homes in Guatemala, Nicaragua, and Honduras. On my first stop at NPH Guatemala, I met ten-year-old Wilmer somewhere between the gigantic main doors and the dining room. Sitting under the shade of a mango tree, his iconic smile beamed as I introduced myself. Immediately, I sensed he had a story to tell. I was amazed that at such a young age, he was able to articulate positive consequences from his tragic accident. He would use comments like, "Yes, it is tragedy, and I wish I were not in this wheelchair. However, without the accident, I would have never learned to read or write, or go the movies, or eat KFC or McDonalds." He projected such gratitude and humility.

Like many young people today, as Wilmer matured with age and wisdom, he started to ask the bigger questions about life, and our conversations grew deeper. Over the years, we pondered topics like the existence of God, why people suffer, and the difference between being spiritual and religious. While we might not have always shared the same point of view or come to the same conclusions, we enjoyed those conversations. After each encounter, I went away respecting his agile mind, his thirst for knowledge and truth, and the ferocity with which he debated these issues. He possessed a beautiful gift—the ability to connect his personal experiences with philosophical issues.

I relished the times we sat under that mango tree—passing time, talking, debating, and dreaming. He was an inspirational thought partner, and my life, like countless others, is better for having known him.

Throughout the years, there have been many moving stories of hope and perseverance to highlight from NPH. This book captures the extraordinary details of Wilmer, who proudly celebrated being part of the NPH family. May his journey from tragedy to triumph inspire you and remind you to never give up.

ACKNOWLEDGMENTS

I'd like to thank:

- The entire Arias family for allowing me to share such a personal story of theirs; and for their invaluable input, without which this story would be incomplete;
- NPH International for the continuous work they do to provide children with better lives;
- My mom for bringing this project to life and helping me see it through;
- My editor Jocelyn Carbonara, and project manager Jenny Lisk;
- Everyone I interviewed during the process of writing—including Marta, Xavier, Jaime, Jacinto, and Yecenia;
- Father Tom Belleque and Donna Egge for introducing my family to NPH; and
- All the workers at all the NPH homes who dedicate their lives to the children.

REFERENCES

Buchholz, Katharina. 2022. "Infographic: Where People Spend the Most & Least Time on Social Media." Statista. April 26, 2022. https://www.statista.com/chart/18983/time-spent-on-social-media/.

Callans, Matthew, and Jacinto Arias. 2020. Personal interview.

Callans, Matthew, and Jaime Cassanova. 2020. Personal interview.

Callans, Matthew, and Marta Garate. 2020. Personal interview.

Callans, Matthew, and Wilmer Arias. 2020. Personal interview.

Callans, Matthew, and Xavier Adsara. 2020. Personal interview.

Callans, Matthew, and Yecenia Arias. 2020. Personal interview.

Hill, Napoleon. 2021. *Think and Grow Rich*. New Delhi: Om SaiTech Books.

"Musonius Rufus Quote: 'You Will Earn the Respect of All If You Begin by Earning the Respect of Yourself. Don't Expect to Encourage Good Deeds in People Conscious of Your Own Misdeeds.'." n.d. Goodreads. Accessed October 20, 2022. https://www.goodreads.com/work/quotes/15962079-musonius-rufus-lectures-and-sayings.

Rodríguez, Eva Maria. 2022. ""'Efecto Bombilla': El Papel Fundamental De La Actitud Para Tener Éxito.'" Edited by Gema Sánchez Cuevas. La Mente Es Maravillosa. October 7, 2022. https://lamenteesmaravillosa.com/victor-kuppers-efecto-bombilla-la-importancia-la-actitud/.

Stoll, Julia. 2022. "U.S. Time Spent Watching Television 2023." Statista. February 14, 2022. https://www.statista.com/statistics/186833/average-television-use-per-person-in-the-us-since-2002/.

Tolle, Eckhart. 2004. *The Power of Now: A Guide to Spiritual Enlightenment*. Berkeley, CA: Publishers Group West.

Vujicic, Nick. 2019. *Life without Limits: Inspiration for a Ridiculously Good Life*. New York, NY: Waterbrook Press.

Wasson, William, Ronald Hicks, and Marlene Farrell Byrne. 2020. *Change the World. Start with the Children*. Chicago, IL: Celtic Chicago, Inc.

ABOUT THE AUTHOR

Matthew Callans is a writer and entrepreneur who lives in Encinitas, California. Upon graduating from Chapman University in 2016, Matthew spent a year in Guatemala volunteering as an English teacher at NPH. Since then, he has cofounded three brands in the health and wellness industry, and is now focused on growing his health supplements brand, Areté Adaptogens, and writing about topics he's passionate about. In his free time, Matthew enjoys surfing, playing the piano, exercising, and reading.

If you'd like to support Matthew's business, please visit AreteAdaptogens.com and use the discount code Wilmer for 15 percent off your first purchase.